THE PORTRAIT OF ECCENTRICITY

THE PORTRAIT OF ECCENTRICITY

Arcimboldo and the Mannerist Grotesque

Giancarlo Maiorino

The Pennsylvania State University Press
University Park and London

Library of Congress Cataloging-in-Publication Data

Maiorino, Giancarlo, 1943–
The portrait of eccentricity:
Arcimboldo and the mannerist
grotesque / Giancarlo Maiorino.

p. cm.
Includes bibliographical references and index.
ISBN 0-271-00727-3 (alk. paper)
1. Arcimboldo, Giuseppe, 1527?–1593—
Criticism and interpretation.
2. Mannerism (Art)—Italy.
3. Grotesque in art. I. Title.
ND623.A7M35 1991
759.5—dc20 90–43219

Printed in the United States of America

It is the policy of The Pennsylvania State University Press to use acid-free paper for the first printing of all clothbound books. Publications on uncoated stock satisfy the minimum requirements of American National Standard for Information Sciences—Permanence of Paper for Printed Library Materials, ANSI Z39.48–1984.

For
my liminal friends
David, Harry, Luis, and Willis.
It has been my lot to be fifth
amid this rowdy bunch at the periphery of comparative eccentricity

Contents

List of Illustrations

Photographic Credits

Archivio Alinari, Florence; Art Resource, New York; Christ Church Library, Oxford; Kunsthistorisches Museum, Vienna; Louvre, Paris; Museum of Decorative Arts, Copenhagen; Photographie Giraudon, Collection Viot, Paris; Skoklosters Slott, Stockholm; Tiroler Landesmuseum Ferdinandeum, Innsbruck; The Toledo Museum of Art, Toledo, Ohio.

Introduction

> *The imagination does not want to end in a diagram that summarizes acquired learning. It seeks a pretext to multiply images . . . for with an "exaggerated" image we are sure to be in the direct line of an autonomous imagination.*
>
> —Gaston Bachelard

I

Whether thematic or monographic, recent studies of Mannerism have centered on panegyrics to artifice (André Pieyre de Mandiargue), curious perspectives (Ernest Gilman), and a variety of stylish styles (John Shearman). A critical consensus has therefore emerged, at least insofar as art pitched mannerist displacements against the centrality of humanist proportion.

In this study, eccentricity is centered on Giuseppe Arcimboldo's bizarre style of portraiture as well as on styles of ludic extravagance. Any interest in the psychology of "odd" Florentines like Piero di Cosimo, Leonardo da Vinci, and Pontormo is therefore excluded.

At arm's length from Saturn's melancholy province, mannerist artists, writers, and theorists cherished figures of eccentricity, which rhetoric made common to the arts. "In rhetoric itself," Ernst R. Curtius has told us, "lies concealed one of the seeds of Mannerism."[1] Seeds grew to maturity during the second half of the sixteenth century, and this interdisciplinary study will focus on a critic-historian (Giorgio Vasari), an artist (Arcimboldo), and a theorist (Gregorio Comanini). I have linked their "praise of the eccentric" to concerns with style, meaning, and cultural significance, all of which gravitate around the mannerist portraiture of eccentricity. On the broader grounds of thematic consistency, my critical approach focuses on the mannerist contextuality of the grotesque, whose very nomenclature is structured on the mimetically ex-centric.

II

Art historians have clarified the extent to which style rested on a strict coordination of knowledge, art, and language throughout the Renaissance. Cicero's approach to periodic style (*Orator*) structured Leon Battista Alberti's treatise *On Painting,* in which narration—the *istoria*—is taken to be the "greatest work of the painter." The rhetoric of oratorical gestures therefore shaped pictorial narratives. A number of critical terms that Leonardo Bruni applied to literature—*figura, colore, lineamenta, forma*—were visual metaphors applicable to painting. Such a lexical fact reflected classical exchanges between literature and art criticism.[2]

Throughout the sixteenth century, John Shearman writes, Ciceronianism and Bembismo were marked by an obsession with style; matter remained "its servant." A willful tendency to shift one language of art toward another led to a systematic "transference of ideals."[3]

III

By 1530, Giulio Camillo's *Della imitazione* acknowledged Cicero as the perfect author who profited from a thousand beauties scattered among his predecessors. That agglutinative idea of merit, Thomas Greene tells us, left "no place for a truly transformative imagination." Camillo, in fact, remained "a collector and an arranger."[4] Under the rubric of "collections," teleological matters of "what" and "why" yielded to quantitative interests in "how much?" Debates on mimesis and originality shifted toward an autonomous realm in which art had to satisfy a culture that relished accumulations of all sorts. Such a "saturated" concept of form was but the inevitable reaction to humanist canons of unsurpassable achievements. The very concept of measure edged on its own defiance during the *Quattrocento.* Erasmian concerns with *copia* were about to spill over into a gargantuan output across the arts.

Even a superficial reading of fifteenth-century panegyrics and art treatises cannot fail to bring out quests for perfection. In the form of virtual accomplishments, Florence had reached the pinnacle of civic excellence in Leonardo Bruni's *Panegyric to the City of Florence* (1403). Likewise, Lorenzo Ghiberti had proclaimed in his *Commentari* that Florentine artists had outdone their classical ancestors. Whereas the ancients "had models to imitate and from which they could learn," Alberti maintained that the moderns could make a greater claim to fame, for they discovered "unheard-of and never-before-seen arts and sciences without teachers or without any model whatsoever."[5] Such enthusiasm steered humanist *aemulatio* toward ideological fulfillment.

One need only mention that Michelangelo on the Sistine ceiling, Raphael in the Stanza della Segnatura, and Castiglione in *The Courtier* created forms of mythic plenitude that brought artistic progress to rest at what Vasari would consider a paradigmatic juncture.[6] At that point, Fame let artists step into the presence of the eternally valid.[7]

On stylistic grounds, Castiglione pinned excellence to Leonardo, Mantegna, Raphael, Michelangelo, and Giorgione: "No one of them appears to lack anything, since we recognize each to be perfect in his own style." In Italian, "perfect" reads "*perfettissimo,*" which puts the highest standard—perfect—into a superlative mode that is logically redundant. Ludovico Ariosto called Michelangelo "Michel more than a man, angel divine" (*Orlando Furioso*), and Varchi later found him to be a "*perfettis simo architettore, eccellentissimo poeta ed amatore divinissimo.*"[8] Hyperbolic accumulations of superlatives quantified perfection into an eclectic cluster of models whose very diversity made each one of them relative and replaceable. The best was not single but plural. Added to the cult of ancient authority (Cicero), the "divine" perfection of modern masters who excelled in a plurality of stylistic forms of expression had to humble even the most ambitious.[9] Perfection became a matter of choice.

By the turn of the *Cinquecento,* emulation had caught up with its own possibilities. Humanist ideology began to fold under the weight of monumental accomplishments that overshadowed past and future. If the Middle Ages were waning north of the Alps, so was Humanism to the south. Those were testing times, and it was easier to hide in dreams and caves than to move outdoors into the daylight. The nocturnal provinces of art gained popularity.[10] *Notturnismo* triumphed in the grottoes of the Boboli Gardens, and Agostino Veneto painted monstrous creatures in his *Trionfo notturno di Ecate.* Anton Francesco Doni and Giovanni Battista Gelli wrote dialogues in uncertain states of wakefulness at a time when Michelangelo and Tasso were trying to mute restless longings in the poetic depths of the night.

Finally, Paolo Lomazzo praised blindness as a source of brighter light:

from Comanini to Lomazzo

> Fuor Talpa e dentro lince
>
> (Outside a mole and inside a lynx)

from Vespasiano Marini to Lomazzo

> Quando mostrò di chiuder gli occhi, aperse
>
> (once blind, he truly opened his eyes)

from Francesco Gallarato to Lomazzo

> E tu, di luci privo
>
> (Mirabil caso, a disegno di stupore)

Apporti chiara luce a tutto il mondo

(And you, although deprived of sight
—Extraordinary case, and worthy of admiration—
Bring clear light to the whole world.)[11]

Such stunning reversals of natural patterns and human conventions betrayed a loss of direction that often led artists to look at the world upside down.

By definition, perfection implied fulfillment, which challenged the progress of art in a very real sense. A fundamental dilemma came to the fore: Could there be an alternative to, or a future after, perfection? Answers ranged from the spiritual unrest of Pontormo and Rosso Fiorentino to the stylistic contentment of Bronzino and Parmigianino. At the same time, Arcimboldo, Buontalenti, and Giambologna undertook experimentations of all kinds.

Matthew Arnold wrote that poets "must begin with an Idea of the world in order not to be prevailed over by the world's multitudinousness."[12] Throughout the *Cinquecento,* ideological losses were compensated by a multitude of styles. Perfection was flanked either by deficiency or excess. The language of the world no longer aimed at unity; instead, it indulged in mesmerizing fragmentations.

IV

The centerpiece of my nomenclature of eccentricity is the bizarre art of Arcimboldo, whose portraits epitomized a cluster of stylistic choices at the periphery of the humanist center. Away from the proportional core of fifteenth-century poetics, eccentricity turned its protean outreach toward figures of excess (chapter 1), rhetorical hyperboles (chapter 2), liminal playfulness (chapter 3), extravagant "outdoing" (chapter 4), grotesque abnormality (chapter 5), and the rhetoric of the Daedalian punster (chapter 6).

Chapter 1 centers on artful tautologies that betrayed leanings toward extravagance in art, literature, and criticism. Vasari's *somma perfezione* and the *sprezzatura artificiosa* of Comanini set "cultural" standards that mapped out rhetoric's impact on Mannerism. Its Lexicon Rhetoricae, to borrow from Kenneth Burke, became the common denominator of the arts. The *homo rhetoricus* often stole the show,[13] and Vasari did not fail to write memorable reviews for posterity.

Chapter 2 takes up Arcimboldo's grotesque portraits, which Roland Barthes made the object of linguistic analysis. I have extended his conclusions to the pictorial language of perspective, a "symbolic form" that Arcimboldo took as a rhetorical metaphor whose ludic core could be stretched beyond any humanist measure.

So far, criticism of Arcimboldo's grotesque portraits has been scanty and divided. While Mario Praz, Gustav René Hocke, and Arnold Hauser place the Milanese artist (1527–93) in the mannerist camp, Eugenio Battisti has moved him to the equally fantastic grounds of *Antirinascimento*. All of them make passing remarks on the painter, whose art well illustrates a penchant for artificial forms of expression.[14] While a consensus still is out of reach, scholarship has not linked the artist to ongoing debates on Maniera and Mannerism. This study takes up that challenge. Arcimboldo's mannerist affiliation on both sides of the Alps was finally vindicated when the show "*Effetto Arcimboldo*" was held in the Venetian Palazzo Grassi during the winter of 1987.[15]

Among the sixteenth-century treatises included in Paola Barocchi's magisterial edition,[16] Comanini's *trattato* stands out for its extensive comments on the art and literature of the age. Direct references are made to Giorgio Vasari, Giulio Romano, and Torquato Tasso, including a long poem on Arcimboldo's portrait of Vertumnus—Rudolph II. I contend in chapter 3 that Comanini's discussion of art theory set eccentricity on liminal grounds where play and parody transgressed the fabric of tradition.

The nomenclature of eccentricity thus stands vis-à-vis the parental heritage of Humanism, which climaxed at the turn of the *Cinquecento* with the High Renaissance of Raphael, Michelangelo, Castiglione, and Machiavelli. I cannot but agree with John

Shearman that Mannerism must be understood in its own historical perspective. While marking grotesque boundaries, the first part of chapter 4 makes three comparisons that are meant to sharpen differences between Mannerism and the Baroque. The first centers on iconography and sets Vertumnus against Proteus. The second focuses on thematology, which takes up the concept of metamorphosis as either mechanical or organic. And the third deals with the maze and the labyrinth as structures symbolic of mannerist and baroque poetics. The second part of the chapter points to mannerist echoes amid the surrealist "fabric of adorable improbabilities." André Breton's phrase is the focus of analogues and borrowings that call for comparisons. To be consistent with the tradition of Italian grotesque, I shall center on Arcimboldo and Giorgio de Chirico. The *gran pittore metafisico,* in fact, paved the way for Surrealism.

Voicing a persistent interest in the works of "surrealists despite themselves,"[17] Tristan Tzara found that "art assumes an axiomatic character" in the "fixed world" of Arcimboldo and Bracelli.[18] Whether it be de Chirico or Dali, the surrealists showed less than a passing interest in Paolo Uccello and Luca Cambiaso; it is by no sheer accident that Man Ray owned a free version of Arcimboldo's *Winter.*[19] Between 1936 and 1939, *Le Minotaure* published essays on themes crucial to the poetics of the grotesque. The collages of Jean Levey were set against four Arcimboldesque canvases (*Seasons, école française du xvi siècle*), and another issue opened with a color reproduction of the Arcimboldesque *L'amiral,* which belonged to the Wolfgang Paalen Collection. Two years earlier, Georges Pudelko took notice of Vasari's belief that Leonardo cherished "all that is curious, extravagant, with a tendency to get lost in play."

Parallels and references of that sort could be quantified. At different points in time, therefore, artists created forms whose structure and expression were strikingly similar. As André Breton wrote, "the marvelous is not the same in every period of history: it partakes in some obscure way of a sort of general revelation only the fragments of which come down to us: they are the romantic *ruins,* the modern mannequin, or any other symbol capable of affecting the human sensibility for a period of time."[20] Along a "continuum" of Western culture, the mannerist grotesque produced an early edition of the vocabulary of surrealist marvels.

In the mode of the grotesque, my critical endeavor traces its path at the surface; it is stylistic and preliminary in nature. It should stir probing studies of the subject, whose playfulness reveals only one of Mannerism's contradictory faces. Such a diachronic leap will also stretch the stylistic range that shoulders my approach to the poetics of the grotesque.

The complexity of Mannerism exceeds the "focused contextuality" of my endeavor, which centers on the grotesque guise of fantastic artforms. To that extent, my methodology follows neither paramount studies of the grotesque nor of Mannerism.[21] Instead, it is lodged between the two, in what I call a "grotesque periphery." To follow James Mirollo's lead, my interdisciplinary approach aims at reconciling the consensus of art historians with the debate of literary critics on matters of periodization.[22]

This study does not treat the grotesque as an ontological category whose validity has become predominant in modern culture. It is for this reason that I do not take up more philosophical concerns, as Geoffrey Harpham does at the beginning and at the end of his book. My outline of a poetics of the grotesque draws from rhetorical forms of eccentricity produced during the sixteenth century.

It is in chapter 5 that I ask, What language does—or would—the grotesque Muse speak? In answering that question, references to Francesco Colonna, Rabelais, Giorgio de Chirico, James Joyce, René Magritte, or Michel Leiris point to their relevance to the genre. By and large, criticism would agree that Colonna and Joyce fall outside the historical parameters of Mannerism, however much we stretch roots and aftermath. Beyond them, one falls back into those "recurrences" that Curtius, Hocke, and Hauser have made us familiar with. Any other claim will be made in the body of the text.

Chapter 6 outlines a playful sketch of the *homo rhetoricus*, whose mannerist roots I have traced back to his mythic locus: the island of Crete.

V

Since grotesque *capricci* and *ghiribizzi* gained strength around the middle of the sixteenth century, Rabelaisian excesses in matters of language, size, and standards of any kind do fall within the chronological province of Mannerism. Without touching on matters of affiliation, this study keeps Rabelais in a position of support. Aspects of his art—as of that of Bruegel, Erasmus, Ronsard, and the Pléiade poets—are taken up only insofar as they "unveil" traits of the culture under discussion, which is centered on Italian Mannerism.

By the same token, I consider matters of "beginnings" more important than concerns with seventeenth-century figures such as Tesauro and Gracián. Gustav René Hocke reminds us that many "formal Mannerisms" were the stock in-trade of the artistic tradition long before the end of the *Cinquecento*.[23] I submit that reactions to, and borrowings from, Alberti and Leonardo claim priority over debates as to whether the grotesque *figuras compuestas* of Francisco de Quevedo in *Los Sueños* echoed either Bosch or Arcimboldo on this bank of the Baroque or at the other side of Mannerism. Either way, mannerist "connections" would call for a different methodology.[24]

VI

The mannerist convergence of art, literature, and theory has made an "intermedia" methodology all the more compelling. Multidisciplinarity cannot but secure a firmer hold on a culture that courted the fantastic in all forms of expression.

Throughout the latter part of the sixteenth century, emblems and metaphorical transfers favored exchanges in the realm of chameleons and *voci dipinte*. While the Horatian concept of *ut pictura poesis* pointed to occasional parallels between art and literature, Arcimboldo set up strict equivalences between sounds and colors. He invented a musical scale based on the pictorial intensity of colors. And his experiments were familiar to Comanini, who also focused on pictorial and poetic "*antiteti*" and "*contraposti.*" Furthermore:

> Èloquente pittura
> È questa, e 'l color muto,
> Ch'aurea bocca figura,
> Dolce risona et è ne' detti arguto.
> Con la viva parola
> Pinge 'l Panigarola
>
> (254)
>
> (This is an eloquent painting,
> Whose mute color
> Represents a golden mouth,
> Whose voice is sweet and whose words are conceited.
> Panigarola is able to paint
> with living words)
>
> (*Trattati,* 3: 370, 360–62)

Painting is a *viva parola,* that is to say, a speaking image replete with linguistic attributes. By the same token, color is taken to speak a mute language. In the ever-popular tradition of *imprese* and literary descriptions of paintings (*ekphrasis*), poetry "showed" and painting "spoke." For the humanists, concordances between art and philosophy updated the resilience of classical and Christian ideas of world harmony. For Arcimboldo and Comanini, instead, the Horatian simile carved an aesthetic vacuum in which capriciousness could mix artforms at will.[25]

In the attempt to keep capriciousness within the bounds of critical discipline, I do expect readers of this book to be somewhat familiar with the "mannerist tangle." I therefore call on them to set up provocative exchanges with this text, whose goal is to promote further inquiries into one's special field of interest.

I believe that my approach ought to be a synthetic one; for me, comparison is an act of synthesis, not of analysis. For me, "how," "what," and "where" are means; "why" is teleological. I therefore try to evaluate "as many modes of human understanding as possible in a single act of the mind." By the same token, I agree with R. P. Blackmur that comparatists, masterlaymen, and their ideological cohorts cannot train "in caution, reserve, and the sin of over-scrupulosity in every matter not directly warranted by fact. It is mere facts that make mere scholarship; it is the mere facts about the work that fail to tell us what the work is about."[26]

Perhaps edging on the higher grounds of aesthetics and the history of ideas, I have chosen to center on leading trends and major developments; particular issues are acknowledged but could not be treated as thoroughly as specialists would be able to. The risk lurking over my shoulder is always that of getting trapped into problems of specific competence that tend to cut into my speculative discourse. My kind of *inter*disciplinary research must weigh quite heavily on the interpretative potential that the *inter*connectedness of artistic forms has to offer. My comparative "mode" must therefore channel individual fields of scholarship into a comprehensive overview unbiased by narrow-minded provincialism. At best, I hope to *offer* leads instead of chasing them. Because of the depth and range that interarts undertakings usually entail, my expository strategy tends to be concise not only by choice but also by need. It is shaped, or at least I like it to be shaped, into a rhetoric whose main thrust lets insights and suggestions branch out toward a plurality of directions.

I do understand that there are times when specialists would like to see more space given to issues raised on their own turf, but I leave it to them to explore those issues further. My task is to lead the reader to take the initiative. To go beyond, I would court incompetence and presumption. If at all successful, my aim is to bring forth an interpretative overview. That way, specialists and comparatists can mark out their respective grounds, maintain a cooperative distribution of labor, and claim competence on a map whose territory would otherwise be too vast for anyone to explore with any credibility.[27]

Part I

Figures of Artificiality

1

Artful Tautologies: The Rhetoric of Excess

Le maniérisme, partant d'une position d'humilité hyperbolisée face au modèle, profite de cette position pour malmener le modèle. . . . Le maniérisme suppose que le système d'opposition établi entre l'allégeance et l'opposition développe des excroissances latérales: proliferation de l'ornamentation rhétorique, hyperbolisation des procédés.

—Claude-Gilbert Dubois

I

In her preface to the study of out-of-size narratives ranging from the miniature to the gigantic, Susan Stewart raises an issue that is both preliminary and programmatic: "What does exaggeration, as a mode of signification, exaggerate?"[1] Since meaning shapes form, her question is crucial to the eccentric poetics of this study.

As a symbolic marker of that mode of signification, Vasari's tautological sequence "a much more absolute perfection—*una molto più assoluta perfezione*" in the preface to the third book of the *Lives* spelled out the linguistic nutshell of much mannerist stylistics. At the start, *una* makes *perfezione* relative; the absolute norm yields a plurality of choices modeled after Raphael, Michelangelo, and Giorgione. For Vasari, even Leonardo's "unfinished" stemmed from endeavors "to add excellence to excellence and perfection to perfection. As our Petrarch has said, the desire outran the performance."[2] Practice no longer found a limit in the highest standard. However unwittingly, the Leonardesque dilemma led the mannerists to believe that perfection could be "outdone." What was conceptually problematic could find a stylistic solution.

Vasari's *molto* is therefore emulative rather than pleonastic, since it triggers a hyperbolic quantification that points the idea-ideal toward production. In the process, *molto* throws perfection to the other side of fulfillment. The noun folds under its own weight. The comparison breaks its own boundaries and spills over; there is too much, and what is left is too little. What emerges is the paradox of an incomparable comparison, which is plausible only because it sustains its own probing intentionality. Exaggeration becomes self-effacing.

Readers ought to be warned that my own critical language at times may sound redundantly smart. The fact is that it is not easy to comment on the mannerist penchant for hyperbolic forms of expression. After all, tautology is a "throwing beyond," an "exaggeration for effect" not to be taken literally. Vasari stretched rhetoric to the limit; proportion had to make room for stylistic excess. While the crescendo "*molto più assoluta*" cut into literal credibility, comparatives and superlatives so inflated meaning that nonsense could easily take over. Playfully, lack of meaning was bracketed between question marks and exclamation points, which also punctuated pride in the craft.

Vasari's tautological bent brought an adjectival point of view to bear on his cherished word: *perfezione*. The *Lives* foregrounds "wholly perfect" (*perfettissimo*), "a not too small perfection" (*non piccola perfezione*), "highest perfection" (*somma perfezione*), and "a much more absolute perfection" (*una molto più assoluta perfezione*). This last phrase is a linguistic buildup that in fact scales value down. What emerges is a procedural excess that could bring perfection within the "marketable" reach of stylistic practice.

Perfection therefore became a point of departure for the mannerists. At its historical birthplace, we find Raphael and Michelangelo, whose Roman masterpieces raised the culture of Humanism to the stasis of plenitude. At an earlier stage, artistic progress had climaxed with the "not immature art" of the Etruscans. Because they were "so perfect," they proved "the existence of an art that was approaching its zenith." Vasari's Florentine biases notwithstanding in the preface to the *Lives,* it was on matters of perfection that language built comparatives and superlatives in the historical aftermath of Raphael and Michelangelo. With an eye to the survival of art as technique, perfection spawned the suffixal filiations of *-ism* and *-esque,* which shifted matter toward manner. At that historical juncture, Lionello Venturi points out, "the public could only move from criticism to panegyrical praise. But what else could the artists do?"[3]

In antiquity, the tautological repetition of words or phrases was a stylistic fault, since meaning had not been altered. When Martianus Capella centered on the "modality" of repetition of the same words, the stylistic fault led to a stylistic figure; the useless became expressive.[4] While hiding the shallowness of meaning, tautology updated the classical view of hyperbole as a straining of truth "for the sake of magnifying or minifying something" (Quintilian, *Institutio Oratoria* viii.6.67). Perfection was blown up into the pyrotechnics of extravagance.

The point is that tautology can be interpretative. Even as simple a repetition as "a father is a father" can disclose a connotative range inasmuch as the first father calls on social and affective relationships. To put it in mythic terms, the tautological structure calls to mind Narcissus, who, Gérard Genette points out, "contemplates in his fountain another Narcissus who is more Narcissus than himself."[5] In his mannerist guise, the youth trades the depth of life for the arabesque of linguistic figures that keep the stillness of readable surfaces undisturbed.

The mannerist vocabulary of *somma, perfettissima, maravigliosa, perfezione* generated a linguistic gigantism that became common to the arts. At all levels, invention went beyond measure; too many details in Arcimboldo's portraits, too large a size in the sculptures at Pratolino and Bomarzo, too much contortion in the giants of Giulio Romano, and much of too much in Rabelaisian literature. Since they had to be "other" than normal by definition, mannerist forms lodged their out-of-size irregularity between humanist economy and baroque abundance.

II

To reconcile matter with mode, Comanini linked *imitazione fantastica* (imitation) to *sprezzatura artificiosa* (expression) (*Trattati,* 3:362). Such an adjectival upgrading of Castiglione's "cultural" ideal overlaid authority with extravagance; the artfully natural became spectacularly artificial. Quintilian would agree that the modern theorist abused rhetoric and "carried" redundancy "to excess" (*Institutio Oratoria* vii.56).

For Castiglione, *sprezzatura* pointed to a mode of behavior aimed at concealing "all art and mak[ing] whatever is done or said appear to be without effort and almost without any thought about it" (43). At issue here is the oxymoron of artful artlessness, a kind of negligent diligence that hides affectation.[6] Ambiguity draws from dissimulation, which would make it possible for individualism to excel amid courtly envy.

In the verses of Psalm 8, the magnificence of creation ("O Lord, our Lord, how glorious is your name over all the earth") mirrors the Lord's name as a sign of his perfection. For the humanist *artifex,* that model was easily applicable to *virtù* and *sprezzatura.* At the end of his book, in fact, Castiglione refers to "that virtue which perhaps among all human things is the greatest and rarest, that is, the manner and method of right rule: which of itself alone would suffice to make men happy and to bring" the Golden Age back to earth (302). The word incorporates the meaning, structure, and method of creativity at its best.

After Cicero and Quintilian, even Gelli, Dolce, and Francisco de Hollanda recommended that art should conceal art (*ars celavit artem*). To unravel such a linguistic riddle, R. J. Clements has pointed to a contextual—or associative and lexical—field of meaning for *sprezzatura:* "Within lightness of touch, easiness of manner, effortless deftness, the semantic value of *sprezzatura* is somewhere in this area."[7] Of the parent verb *sprezzare–disprezzare* (to disdain), *sprezzatura* upholds the presumption of a righteous superiority vis-à-vis anything different. Consistent with the humanist bent of mind, Castiglione used *sprezzatura* in conjunction with *disinvoltura*, "*sprezzata disinvoltura*" (44). At once outreaching and exclusive, *sprezzatura* voiced a mythic potential for perfection.

Virtù, sprezzatura, grazia, and *terribilità* blended individual talent with public expectations. Precision was lost to a semantic elusiveness in which nestled the very secret of excellence, whose clusterlike attributes could be neither "translated" nor "explained" without vilifying its rarity.[8] Short of any utopian epiphany, the potential for mixture, conjunction, and hybridism was there.

On matters of definition, Petrarch had already understood that "there is a mysterious something," the quality of which "is to be felt rather than defined."[9] Alberti added that "perhaps the first thing necessary is not so much either virtue or riches, but a certain something for which I cannot find a name, which attracts men and makes them love one person more than another."[10] The excess of meaning over definition was innate to a vocabulary that also uttered the excess of aspirations over results.[11] However linked to what took place in Florence, Urbino, and Rome, *virtù* and *sprezzatura* were the verbal symbols of a society in which knowledge had woven feeling, thought, rhetoric, and tone into a moral style that took on playful guises once it crossed the mannerist threshold.[12]

At its very inception, *sprezzatura* stood at the core of an ideal courtier who was to assert excellence and tame ostentation. As such, *sprezzatura* worded a godlike plurality of talents whose nature—and function—had to remain exceptional. Much of its indeterminacy rested with an emulative potential about to surpass itself: "He who performs well with so much facility must possess even greater skill than this, and that, if he were to devote care and effort to what he does, he could do it far better" (46). Since *molto maggiore* and *molto meglio* led language to exaggerate its meaning, expression edged on tautology. While the "what" was ignored, the "how" was foregrounded; at least hypothetically, the best could be better, so that perfection itself would be emulated in excess of its axiomatic completeness.

On the subject of dance, Castiglione wrote that "masquerading carries with it a certain freedom and license, which among other things enables one to choose the role in which he feels most able, and to bring diligence and a care for elegance into that principal aim, and to show a certain nonchalance ("*una certa sprezzatura*") in what does not matter" (103). Article ("*una*") and adjective ("*certa*") inflate indeterminacy, which verges on hyperbole once it links up to the elusive noun. On the stage, the artificial movements of dance are to be "artified" through a role-playing that tones down the very subject of the performance; manner has emptied matter out. Excess brought perfection within a "modal" reach at the other side of the concept itself. Mannerism returned to the realm of practice what Humanism had raised to ideal heights. The shift from one to the other calls for comments.

III

The ancient contention that "nothing is completed at the beginning" (Seneca, *Naturales Quaestiones*) was rooted in the natural condition of things, and stood against forms of heroic adulthood. Undoubtedly Alberti was aware of such a twofold heritage when he equated origin with maturity in his treatise on painting:

> I was pleased to seize the glory of being the first to write of this most suitable art. If I have been little able to satisfy the reader, blame nature no less than me, for it imposes this law on things, that there is no art which has not had its beginnings in things full of errors. Nothing is at the same time new born and perfect—*nulla si truova insieme nato e perfetto*. (98)

In fact, Alberti echoed Cicero: "Nothing has ever yet been invented and perfected at the same time—*nihil est enim simul et inventum et perfectum*" (*Brutus*). Since it comes at the very end of *On Painting* (*De pictura* 1435–36), acceptance of the natural process could not be taken literally without discrediting the model that had just been set up. On the contrary, the treatise is built on a measure of self-confidence averse to belated confessions of inadequacy. Rhetorical allowances aside, Alberti took on the classical precept at the very beginning of his theoretical work: "I believe the power of acquiring wide fame in any art or science lies in our industry and diligence more than in the times or in the gifts of nature" (39). Like other humanists, he challenged the limits ("has ever yet") that the external world places on human potential.

By the turn of the sixteenth century, even the gods contributed their best talents to the forging of Machiavelli's Ideal Ruler. Moreover,

> in that earth mingled with water such a spirit
> Minerva put as time or labor never produces.
> (*On Ambition*, 82–83)

At birth, the humanist Minerva bestowed her flawless maturity on excellent men. At death, Pietro Bembo so phrased Raphael's epitaph:

> *Hic ille est Raphael, metuit quo sospite vinci*
> *rerum magna parens, et moriente, mori.*

> (Here lies Raphael, in whose lifetime the great Mother of things feared to be outdone, and at his death, feared to die.)

While nature endures through art, only the artist stands at the threshold between time and eternity,[13] where the Albertian treatises on the arts and on the family set up models of a utopian geometry. Growth and experience yielded to a body of artistic rules "worthy of consuming all our time and study." Painting truly "makes the dead seem almost alive." An aesthetic ideal aimed at "building anew an art about which nothing . . . has been written in this age" (*O.P.*, 63–65) was to reconstruct life on a Parnassian mountaintop where the ego shaped images of its own making.

The humanist nomenclature rested on the superlative, and language molded perfection into a verbal theory of knowledge. Even Platonic rhetoric spelled "the best of human things," since there is nothing "greater than the word" that persuades "senators, judges, and citizens" (*Gorgias,* 341–43). Furthermore, "not every man is able to give a name but only the maker of names; and this is the legislator" (*Cratylus,* 389). The union of reason with language would generate art, laws, nations, and culture itself. In turn, the humanist inscribed his self-contained cosmos of ideal forms in the autonomy of the word. As a legislator, he created a norm, its object, and the pattern of order harmonizing them.

At the very outset of *On Painting,* Alberti regrets that "so many excellent and superior arts and sciences from our most vigorous antique past could now seem lacking and almost wholly lost" (39). The initial qualification implies the superlative "*ottime,*" which exceeded the "*nobilissimi e maravigliosi intelletti*" of the ancients. What follows is a kind of transcendental exaggeration by means of attributes such as "divine," which would be bestowed on Leonardo, Raphael, and Michelangelo. In the realm of humanist culture, the rhetoric of excellence was an ideological imperative.

It is indicative that Alberti first refers to the ruins of antiquity, and then praises Filippo Brunelleschi's majestic cupola of S. Maria del Fiore, which in turn frames the literary architecture of the treatise. Initial echoes of Pliny and Greek epigrammatic eulogies in which nature gave its best in bringing to life "geniuses or giants" yield to a recognition of modern talents capable of accomplishing "every praiseworthy thing." At the end of the book, exceptional efforts give way to a Florentine progeny whose theoretical knowledge could indeed "make painting absolute and perfect" (*O.P.*, 39, 98).

While finding initial encouragement in the works of Masaccio, Donatello, Luca della Robbia, Ghiberti, and Brunelleschi, Alberti ends with a statement of faith in theoreticians. If at all needed, his "successor" would be a theorist "helpful to painters" and capable of making "this noble art well governed" (*O.P.*, 98). The last two words of the treatise are adjectives that qualify the art of painting as absolute and perfect: "*assoluta e perfetta*." At such heights, excellence was about to grow out of its own achievements.

The preface to *On Painting* names the great masters of the first humanist generation, but the rest of the treatise makes references only to the ancients. At the end, a "rhetorical Other" would legitimize theory as perfection. The rhetoric of Humanism in fact was lodged in the superlative standards of treatises and panegyrics that voiced fulfillment. At best, enthusiasm was restrained into forms of aloof serenity.

Once the historical crisis of Humanism began to escalate, leanings toward either loss or exaggeration intensified. From Cellini's *Vita* to the *Lives* of Vasari, many threw personal fervor and linguistic audacity beyond measure; they often tampered with restraint, and rhetoric gave them tools for doing so. Since at issue here is the demonstrative rhetoric of praise (*Rhetorica ad Herennium* iii.6.10), it is worth noting that Ernst Curtius views the trope of hyperbole as a case of "outdoing" typical of panegyrics and art treatises.[14]

As it happened, the mannerists took either lateral or parodic stands toward their humanist heritage. Without carrying any ideological critique, their "misreadings" steered trust in theory toward confidence in their mastery of technique. At the other side of the last humanist accomplishments, the mannerists found the impossible, the wishful, and the excessive. Tautology broke free of empirical restraints and *perfezione* was qualified as *somma*.[15] Excess thrived on its own dynamics, gaining strength from its tautological thrust.

IV

For the mannerist, tautology was more than a rhetorical figure. As a "needless repetition," it made a welcomed spectacle of itself;

as a stylistic choice, it favored an approach to art that affected form, content, and tradition. Vasari fitted invention into the referential mold of a hyperbolic language which so saturated meaning that concerns with expression became exclusive.[16]

In classical rhetoric, hyperbole is "a manner of speech exaggerating the truth" (*Ad Herennium* iv.33), or "an elegant straining of truth" (Quintilian, *Institutio Oratoria* viii.6.67). Emphasis is placed on a manner that exceeds normality. And Erasmus later added that its abnormality implied an epistemological reversal whereby hyperbole "says more than the situation warrants, yet the truth can be inferred from the falsehood." He even tried to make "the superlative more emphatic" through verbs, adverbs, positive adjectives modified by an adverb, and periphrases (*De copia* i.28.44–47, written in 1512–14).

Writing on stylistic matters of redundancy, Erasmus defended "poetic liberties of almost any kind." There were places where standards were reversed. The popular objection carried the day, and autonomy of style legitimized license, which Horace could not let go "beyond the point of associating what is wild with what is tame." Artists who favored tropes of excess violated that limit with a passion. In a superficially rhetorical sense, Erasmus's "exercises to develop the powers of expression" unwittingly read as a mannerist index: "compressed and abundant style," "variety," "heightening," "hyperbole," "making the superlative more emphatic," "varying the expression of the superlative," "virtuoso practical demonstration." The aim was to endow artists with a rhetorical "godlike power." By the same token, prolixity in matters of style could pile up "a meaningless heap of words and expressions without any discrimination." He even caught Cicero indulging in the excessive verbosity of "the florid" Asian style:

> Once we have carefully committed the theory of memory, we should frequently take a group of sentences and deliberately set out to express each of them in as many versions as possible, as Quintilian advises, using the analogy of a piece of wax which can be moulded into one shape after another. . . . We shall find it particularly useful to "thumb

> the great authors by night and day," especially those who were outstanding in the rich style, such as Cicero, Aulus Gellius, and Apuleius. We must keep our eyes open to observe every figure of speech that they use, store it in our memory once observed, imitate it once remembered, and by constant employment develop an expertise by which we may call upon it instantly. (*De copia* i.1.4, 9)

The models of the artistic tradition are like wax to be shaped into new forms.

For Walter Pater, the centrifugal tendency of the Asiatic stirs curiosity in the guise of an "endless play of undirected imagination"; the Attic, instead, is centripetal in its Dorian pursuit of "severe simplification everywhere." Tensions between rule and license, imitation and curiosity, were to keep both approaches in check. When curiosity is deficient, academism settles in, and a mannerist case would be Jacopino del Conte. When curiosity "is in excess," one is liable "to be satisfied with what is exaggerated in art."[17] At the mannerist frontier, idealization gave way to artificiality.

While flaunting the superlative, hyperbole—like tautology—pointed to an artistic program. In his comments on Aristotle's *Poetics* vis-à-vis emotional utterances in speech (*Rhetoric* iii.7), Gerald Else relates "figures" to "feeling-states." Tautology was taken to be a figure of speech that would be valued "not so much in the technical sense, i.e. manipulations of language *per se,* as in the broader sense of *modes of the expression of feeling* in language."[18] Whether its models were Cicero, Petrarch, Raphael, or Michelangelo, the mannerist nomenclature of excess turned them into rhetorical standards that restricted the expression of feelings to playfulness.

V

By the end of the sixteenth century, *sprezzatura* became *artificiosa.* At first Comanini's tautological compound seems to magnify the "sameness of meaning." Yet redundancy is so deliberate that it calls for interpretation. To begin with, Castiglione's *sprezzatura* was a charismatic talent measured up to a model "without defect of any kind" (11) in a book meant to "[form] in words a perfect Courtier" (25). Without entering the utilitarian language of court, such a standard foreshadowed ways in which the archetypal Courtier would act if he could ever come to life. That possibility was denied by the text's retrospective point of view, which kept *sprezzatura*'s actual performance virtual.

Regardless of social instructions, *sprezzatura artificiosa* centered on artistic effects; the adjective turned definition—*sprezzatura, perfezione*—into procedure. Relevant at this point are S. I. Hayakawa's comments on the expression "business is business after all." What appears to be a simple statement of fact "is not simple and is not a statement of fact. The first business denotes the transaction under discussion; the second business invokes the connotations of the word. The sentence is a directive, saying, Let us treat this transaction with complete disregard for considerations other than profit."[19] Likewise, the mannerist tautologies of Comanini and Vasari are directives as assertive as any effort to repeat/quote/parody/caricature. The tautological moment is not inventive but digressive. It manipulates what tradition has to offer.

Consistent with the mannerist penchant for mimetic disguises and perspectival tricks, tautology, Gilles Deleuze would agree, foregrounds *différence* more than *répétition;* actually, one is a vehicle for the other. Any structure of sameness implies a gap, since analogy presumes a break between similarity and identity. Even the archetypal resemblance between man and God rests on a qualitative difference.

All tropes touch on distance, which, however wide (metaphor) or narrow (simile), does weigh on meaning. Like other tropes, tautology makes a commentary; the very act of reiteration adds "quotation marks" and leans toward clichés and "isms." Because it aims at a deliberate effect, tautology might not touch on truth, but it does not fail to affect style by favoring rhetoric over epistemology.[20]

Adjectival (*somma*) qualifications of *perfezione* in fact disqualified it as an absolute. In the same negative mode of "art that does not seem to be art," meaning is built by destroying it. At issue here is the paradoxical attempt to set up some kind of absolute standard for the unique or perfect genius. As a transgressive marker, originality of style falls beyond conformity to models of perfection.[21]

Mannerist tautology thus set to work an adjectival reduction that made it possible for perfection to invalidate itself. The result was imperfection, which fell within the reach of artistic practice. Even as conservative a critic as Cardinal Paleotti "legitimized" the dialogic of excess and reduction. In fact, perfection became an adjective, while imperfection claimed the rank of noun. The result was oxymoronic: "*imperfezzione perfetta.*" As an adjective, perfection came to qualify a manner whose substantial "imperfection" brought it within reach of production. By the same token, "*diminuzione con augmento*" (*Trattati,* 2:381) implies a gesture without substantive changes. Excess took on itself, reversing matter into *maniera.*

The word "artificial" (*artificiosa*) does mean unnatural, crafty, manufactured, and simulated, effects that the noun (*sprezzatura*) conceals but the adjective flaunts. However conscious of the fact that one root of *maniera* is the Latin *manus,* that is to say, made by hand, the adjectival manner has caused a reversal in the grammatical hierarchy. Much like an overgrown parasite, the adjective has almost swallowed the noun's meaning and function.

To illustrate the topicality of mannerist concerns with style, we ought to take notice of Paul Valéry's brief note on the subject. What was born from a technical instrument, the *stylus,* soon became symbolic: "Thus style signifies the manner in which a man expresses himself, regardless of what he expresses. . . . It is in the act of expression that the man distinguishes himself." Style is act, thriving on "an active faculty of simulation and dissimulation which sometimes becomes dominant." Here we move back into the ambiguous realm of artless artfulness. Like *sprezzatura,* style "means something more than manner of being or doing, and this 'something' is not easily defined." Perhaps that something is a field of tautological ambiguity in which style is manner that means more than manner itself. It is a something that is not enough, and its better "Other" eludes words. The tautological impulse is there, but the linguistic vehicle is inadequate. The rhetorical figure points toward a performance-act that itself amounts to a "stylistic" interpretation of the concept. To Valéry's dismay, *stylus* as technique could inflate the act of expression: "Untempered caprice . . . extravagance and eccentricity" can reduce "a good style" to a "mechanical or imitable fabrication."[22] And much mannerist praxis led to *imitazioni delle maniere*,[23] that is to say, imitations of the imitable.

VI

On the referential grounds of the mannerist experience, *somma perfezione* and *sprezzatura artificiosa* exploited the "historical" gap between noun and adjective. As a variation of in-the-manner-of, the adjective teased the substantive, muting anxiety into vogues that unleashed freedom of craft for its own sake. In the "historical" gap, the adjective released a stylistic potential that was either curbed or dormant in the referent.

On such grounds, Camillo Pellegrino, author of *Il Carafa, o vero della epica poesia,* found that Ariosto had been outclassed by Tasso, who could create new forms of writing and more artful modes of elocution: "*Nuovi modi di dire e locuzioni più artificiose.*"[24] *Inventio* turned *elocutio* into a referential language that was at once a metalanguage of artificial exaggerations of the "Other"—whether he be Petrarch, Bembo, Michelangelo, or Raphael—and a sublanguage on account of its imitative stand in front of it. Either way, such a rhetorical *altérité* played at the margins of both progress and tradition. As an artificial counterpart to humanist analogy, mannerist tautology shifted matters of authorial "anxiety" toward ludic misreadings.

To follow Harold Bloom, hyperbole and tautology are tropes for influence. Accordingly, *sprezzatura artificiosa* and *somma perfezione* would be metaleptic, for they involve "influence as a composite trope for interpretation." The metaleptic trope is "a trope-reversing trope, a figure of a figure";[25] like Arcimboldesque portraits, it finds the same in the other, and vice versa.

Within the self-enclosed activity of what has been called agonistic antagonism ("*antagonismo agonistico*"), the mannerist approach to tautology upset the fabric of language in much the same way as the grotesque altered the integrity of mimetic forms. Perhaps it was not by accident that Rhetoric was depicted as an overdressed woman whose excessive makeup was meant to invite a particular sort of attention.[26]

At the ancestral *Ur* point of regressive indebtedness, Mannerism found Raphael and Michelangelo. The progress of art did not follow the progress of ideas. Instead, stylistic options prevailed; theory and practice made digression as relevant as the "source," and the *ekphrases* of Vasari and Comanini became almost as meritorious as the artworks they described.

VII

At the center of the humanist fabric of knowledge, there stood the noun, which spelled the values of the cultural process. And there stood *virtù*, *grazia*, and *sprezzatura*. With the mannerists, the noun became adjectival and made a spectacle of itself; it became playful and hyperbolic. In its adjectival form, therefore, definition yielded to modality.

Vincenzo Danti finally sanctioned the shift from the adjectival to the adverbial, which steered perfection into the guise of its own "repetitive manner." Having prefaced his treatise on perfect proportions with a reference to Michelangelo's "*eccellente perfezzione*" (*Trattati*, 1:211), Danti then proceeded to see the artist as an "*artefice*" whose "*perfezzione di artifizio*" departed from a "*semplice e naturale pratica*." The execution of the artwork stemmed from the artful manner of craftsmanship. Form was a "*composto*" of ideas lodged "*perfettamente*" in the mind and brought out "*perfettamente*" by hands capable of dealing with imitation "*perfettamente*." Unlike painting and sculpture, architecture could achieve a "*molto maggior artifizio e perfezzione*" (ibid., 237), since its *maniera* was free of mimetic restrictions. So endowed, artificer and artifact could conquer the "*artifiziale teorica*" (ibid., 265–67).

Mannerist language thus foregrounded the concept, manner, and standard of a hyperbolic nomenclature in which artifice edged on ideology. The adverbial mode toned down teleological concerns, so that perfection brought out forms of a "mannered" understanding of its own potential. Without inhibitions, art rejoiced in the ostentation of styles of excess.[27]

2

Arcimboldo's Panegyric to Artifice: The Language of Perspective as a Rhetorical Metaphor

Dimmi come ti configuri rispetto alla retorica e ti dirò chi sei.
—Renato Barilli

I

In Arcimboldo's hands, the stylistics of both excess and eccentricity affected even as mimetic a genre as portraiture. His *Seasons* (four canvases, 1566) are straight profiles, yet they combine the flatness of two-dimensional outlines with the shallow depth of volumetric details whose very abundance hinders their own integrity. Such an excessive accumulation of forms betrayed a grotesque bent of mind that fused—and confused—portraiture, landscape, and still life. In spite of an extravagant assemblage of natural and artificial objects, Arcimboldo's profiles are set against aperspectival backgrounds. The shapes making up the anatomical whole preserve their depth, but the predominant effect is that of a crowded plane on which shallowness of foreground and flatness of middle and backgrounds test ambiguity.

At the edge between the surface values of planimetric outlines and the depth of volumetric details, Arcimboldo carved a pictorial realm in which he could manipulate idea and reality without committing himself to either one.[1] Since theorists and patrons alike stated a preference for the unusual, artists toyed with spatial equivocations. Originality fostered experimentation with lovely as well as unsightly forms. Arcimboldo's "archipelago" heads could indeed bestow mannerist pride on the *pittore misto,* a maker of the marvelous whom G. A. Gilio entrusted with mixing "real and false things" (*Trattati,* 3:16). Reality could be multiplied many times over in the bottomless maze of the mind, where the demons of fantasy courted the hybrid proliferations of irregularity.[2]

One after the other, Arcimboldo's grotesque figures show forth details that link up to the given titles; leafless branches do make up *The Winter* (1563; Fig. 1). The result is a double illusion. Nature appears humanlike, while the natural but unhuman parts of the face shape a kind of physiological presence. At a time when Leonardo had exploited distortion and monstrosity in his drawings of "odd" human specimens, when Giambologna was sculpting a variety of animals in bronze and Caravaggio was about to present a basket of fruit as a legitimate subject in painting, Arcimboldo fell back on the humanist subordination of nature to man. Whether in the form of *Elements* (1563), *Seasons,* or *Human Professions* (1574), he could look at reality only through the human figure. Because it toyed with irregularity and mimesis alike, his bizarre approach heightened the interplay between falsity and probability.

II

The humanist system of linear perspective turned objects into proportional forms whereby bark and cloth, tree trunk and leg,

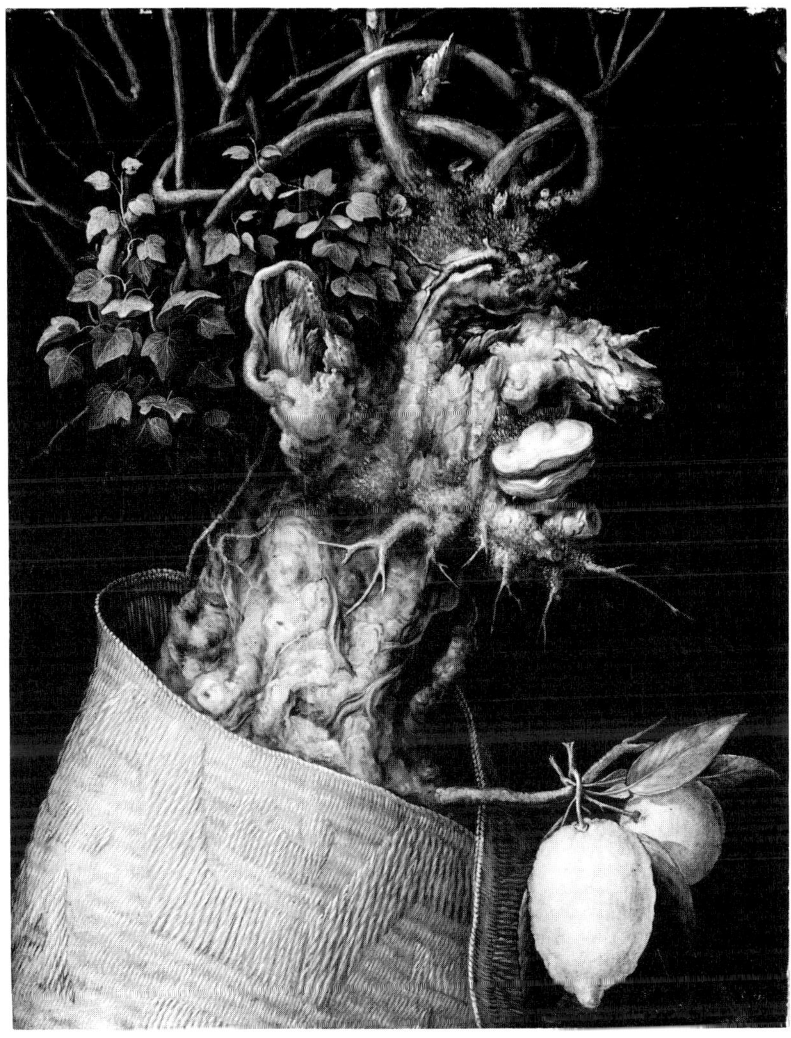

Fig. 1. Giuseppe Arcimboldo, *The Winter*, 1563. Kunsthistorisches Museum, Vienna

garland and circle, share a relational homogeneity, as in Piero della Francesca's *Baptism of Christ* (1440–50). Arcimboldo also made it possible for animals and vegetables to form a nose as long as their shapes were anatomically acceptable. To quote Roland Barthes, he never tired of using "different forms to represent the same thing. Does he want to paint a nose? His multitude of synonyms proposes a branch, a pear, a pumpkin, corn, flowers, fish."[3] Interest is centered neither in the fish nor in the nose alone, but in teasing the very concept of reciprocity; every form is *like* and *unlike* other forms. Similitude became a Janus-like concept, and precedence was given to metaphorical effects.

Extravagance inspired Arcimboldo, who, in *The Man and the Vegetables* (Figs. 2, 3), held objects hostage to directional shifts. By exploiting duplicity and reversibility, the artist makes of the canvas at once a grotesque portrait and a still life. However abstract, linear perspective accepted space as the gravitational link between man and reality. For Arcimboldo, instead, the only center of gravity was his own mind, in which eccentricity reigned supreme. It was a time when the Copernican revolution unsettled earth-centered views of the universe, and one could hardly blame art for not fixing one.

Transgressions of all sorts fed the imagination, and an emergent poetics of surprise stormed the arts. To stir wonder, artists made of the unexpected a predominant mode of artistic invention. Giacomo Zanguidi, known as Bertoia, frescoed a crowded hall with columns made of transparent glass in Palazzo del Giardino (Parma, 1566–71), and Michelangelo placed double columns into the wall in the vestibule of the Biblioteca Laurenziana (Florence, 1524–34), whose Vasarian staircase (1555–68; Fig. 4) flows downward like melting lava. While internal and external spaces were mixed in Vasari's own Ninfeo of Villa Giulia (Rome, after 1552; Fig. 5), grottolike effects in Giulio Romano's Sala dei Giganti in Palazzo del Tè in Mantua (finished 1534; Fig. 6) uprooted the support function of ceiling and walls. Furthermore, half-windows along the base line of his Mantua house give the strange impression that the whole building is about to sink into the ground. In Villa d'Este (Tivoli, near Rome, 1566–69), Pirro Ligorio directed the construction of

Fig. 2. Giuseppe Arcimboldo, *The Man and the Vegetables*. Museo Civico, Cremona

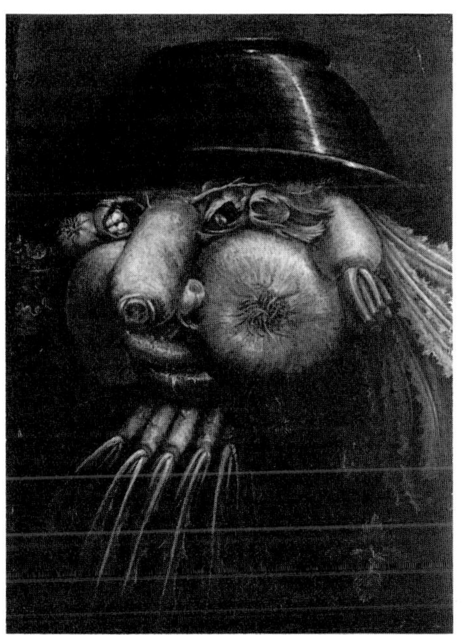

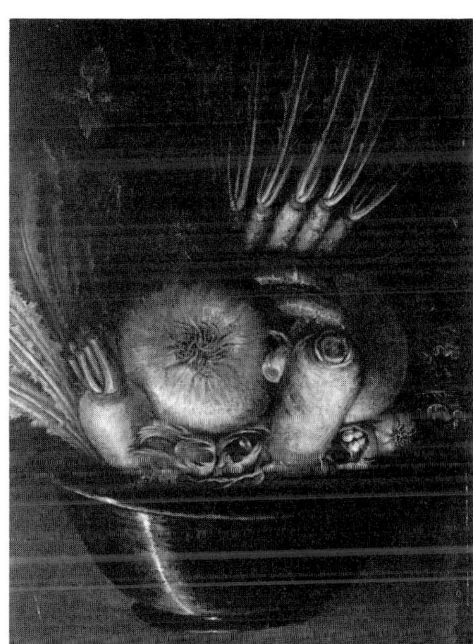

Fig. 3. Giuseppe Arcimboldo, *The Man and the Vegetables* (upside down)

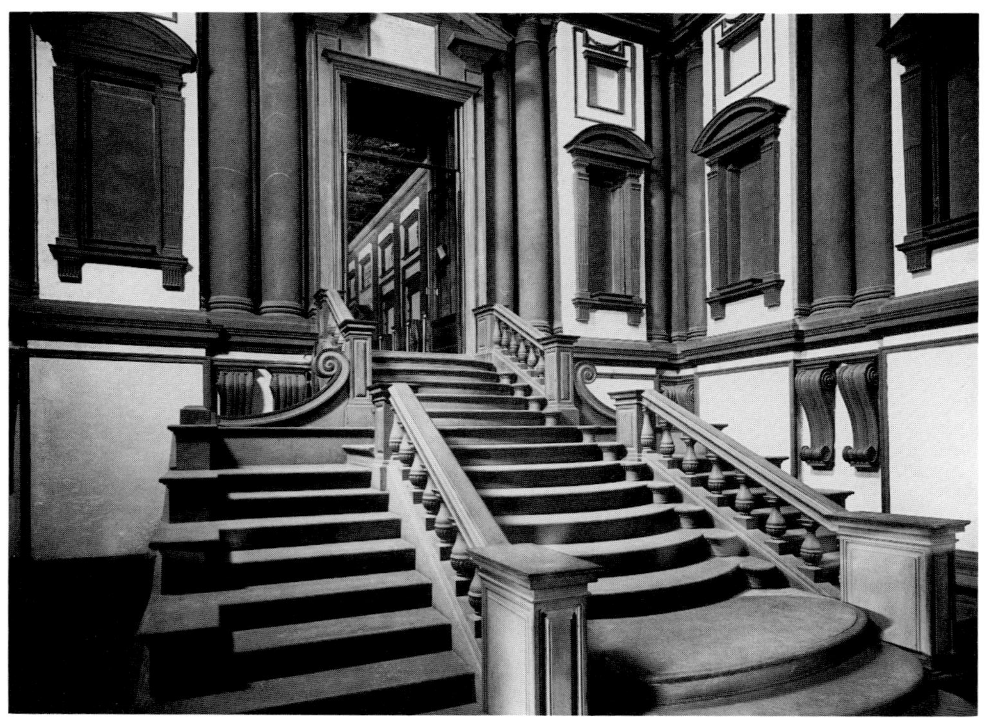

Fig. 4. Michelangelo, vestibule of the Laurentian Library, with Vasari's staircase, 1555–68. Florence

grottoes that were raised to the ground floor, whereas the cavelike walk by the Water Organ led people through rain showers of an artificial meteorology.[4]

Perception was unsettled beyond plausibility, and the very notions of up and down lost much of their bearing. Leonardo da Vinci led the way toward perspectival eccentricity when he made the first anamorphic sketches of a child's head and of an eye. Perspectival exercises of that sort fostered monstrous irregularities. At first Leonardo and Dürer used anamorphosis as a technical curiosity, but it quickly became an effective tool for producing optical distortions and a philosophy of false reality that displaced the humanist symbolism of linear perspective as a form of intellectual certainty. Trompe l'oeil and anamorphoses turned perspective into what Gustav René Hocke has called "perspectivism" (*Perspektivismus*).[5] Because it attempts to phrase the epistemological vacuity of form as content and of content as form, such an ambiguous term points to the visual distortions of a ludic frame of mind.

In terms of Arcimboldo's pictorial syntax, parts are predominant close by, while the whole stands out at a distance. What emerges is a double language, simultaneously clear and obscure. Whatever the viewer's distance from them, his figures always favor reversibility; the fish shows forth the nose, which undoubtedly consists of a fish. Image and meaning therefore fluctuate between optical vision and intellectual discrimination. Likewise, the large masses of rocks that make up Giambologna's Apennine god at Pratolino (near Florence; Fig. 7) are effective at a distance but vanish into a gigantic amount of details close by. At once participant and interpreter, the viewer fell hostage to rhetorico-perspectival puns. Artworks were aimed at pleasure, which soon spawned a rather playful self-complacency that enforced Castelvetro's theoretical emphasis on *delectare* over *docere*.[6]

III

Turning our focus to shifts between literal and conceptual levels of meaning, Arcimboldo's *The Water* (1566; Fig. 8) presents a

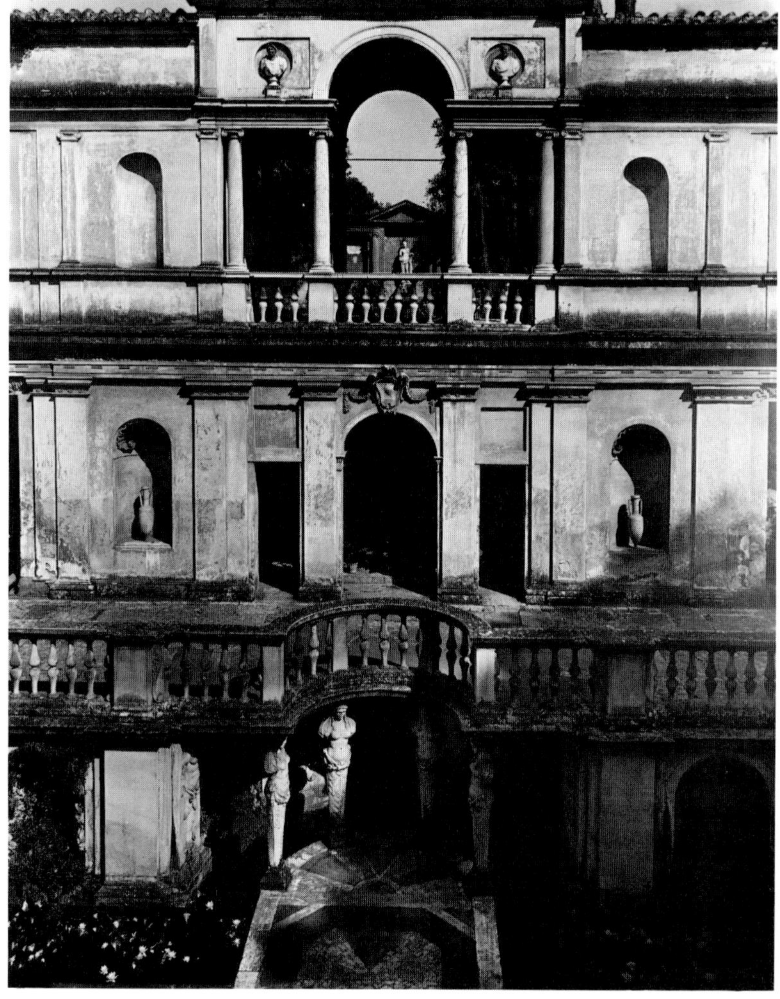

Fig. 5. Giorgio Vasari, Ninfeo, after 1552. Villa Giulia, Rome

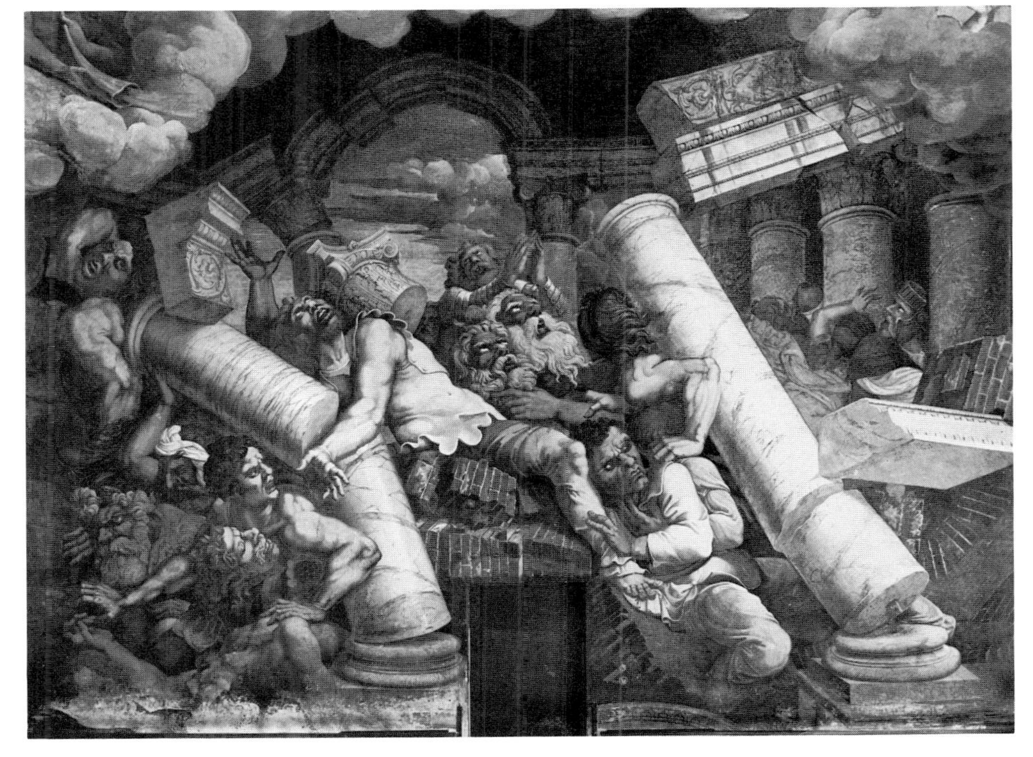

Fig. 6. Giulio Romano, *The Fall of the Giants*, 1531–35. Palazzo del Tè, Mantua

bust constructed with a cornucopian assemblage of sea fauna. The subject is at once illustrated through the perception of the whole portrait at a distance and then denied by the predominance of individual parts close by. The human profile standing between the particular and the general outlines a double-edged metaphor. Each shape therefore carries a double truth: as itself and as part of the anatomy. Personification rested with mechanisms of transfer that unsettled the grammar of visibility. Just as individual words are polysemous, so pictorial details could mean one thing but function as another.[7] Their semantic stability was challenged beyond the bounds of plausible denotations. Fish and water—that is, object and idea—teased both relationship and exclusion.

Roland Barthes writes that whenever a fish forms either a nose or a mouth (*The Water*) Arcimboldo makes use of *antanaclasis,* a rhetorical figure in which a word is repeated with a different meaning. Likewise, *annomination,* which evokes a thing through another of the same form, comes into play when the hind side of a rabbit is shaped like a nose (*The Earth*). In his own way "Arcimboldo is a rhetorician" and his canvases are "a real laboratory of tropes."[8] *The Water* so crowds fish and seashells that the grammar of visual contiguity becomes quite akin to the deletion of rhetorical links by means of the asyndethon, which forces the reader to jump from one detail to the next. Arcimboldo also took advantage of synecdoche, a rhetorical figure in which a part stands for the whole, as in the case of flowers and dried roots that symbolize summer and winter. The arts exploited techniques of accumulation and substitution.

Representing the action or product instead of the agent, *The Fire* (1566; Fig. 9) is metonymic inasmuch as a bunch of burning twigs makes up the portrait's hair. If the fire-man is the agent, the lighted wick is the product, which in turn produces fire; through the incandescent metaphor, metonymy has run its course. Yet, pistols and cannons also generate a play on words that pivot on the Italian *fuoco* (fire) and *armi da fuoco* (firearms). Here *paronomasia* generates a ludic approach to etymology, which links the modernity of firearms to primitive acts of technological ingenuity still associated with fire. Fuses, fire, and

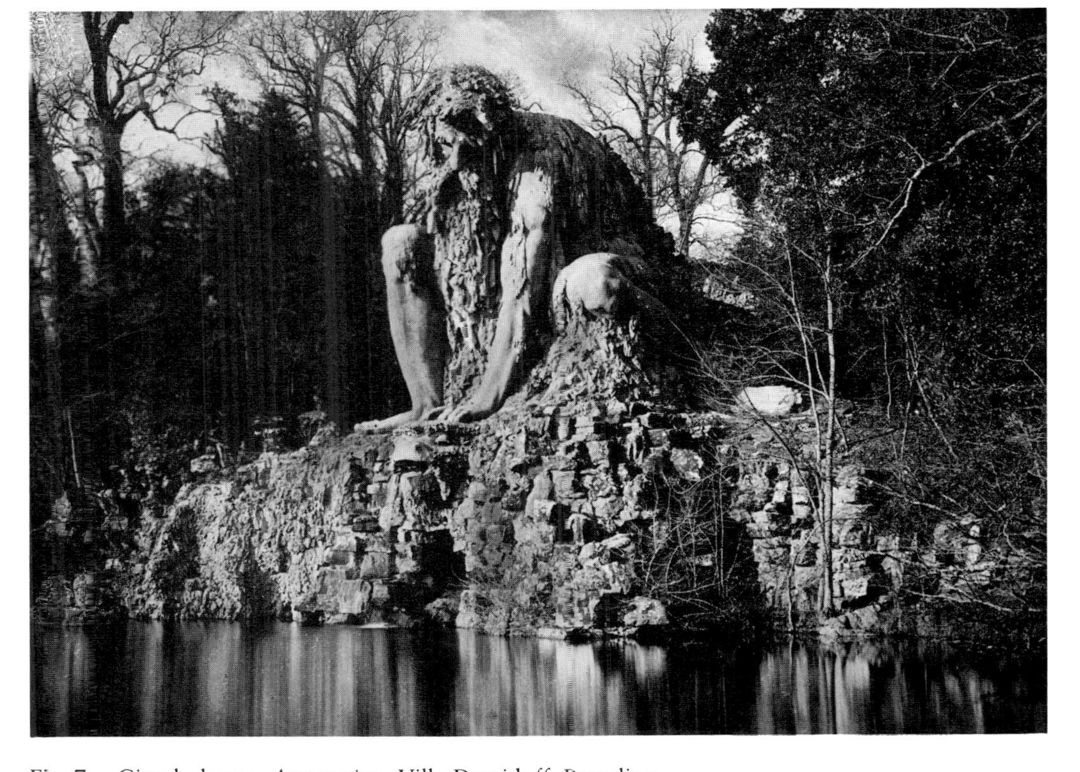

Fig. 7. Giambologna, *Appennino*. Villa Demidoff, Pratolino

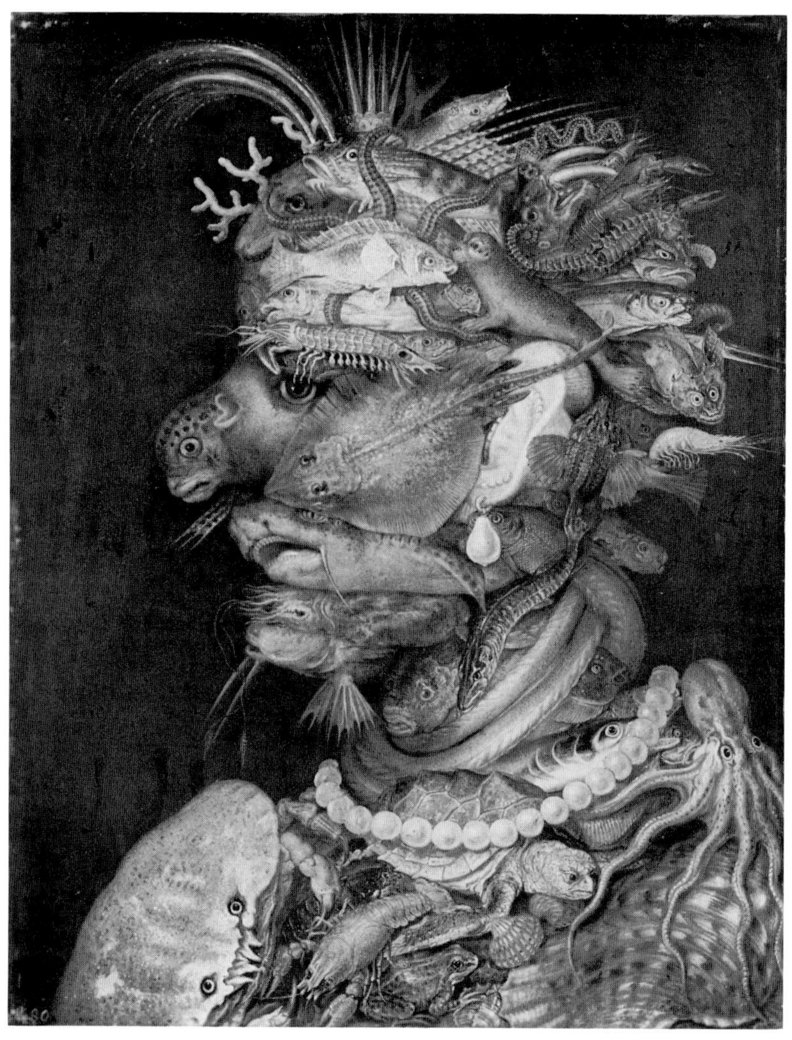

Fig. 8. Giuseppe Arcimboldo, *The Water,* 1566. Kunsthistorisches Museum, Vienna

firearms are drawn into the picture through psycholinguistic layers of meaning that tend to link causes to effects. While metonymy finds a limit in the evidence of the external world, metaphors test the resources of invention. To keep pace with the subject matter, meaning is expanded into a conflagration of details that mark a nutshell history of fire as an archetypal form of weaponry. At a rhetorical level, Derek Attridge would suggest, the title and meaning of the canvas are both a diachronic word-history and a synchronic word-play.[9] To his heart's delight, Arcimboldo mingled them in such a way that neither emerged as predominant.

Metonymy keeps the effects of a fateful decision within the head itself in the Arcimboldesque *Herod's Head* (Fig. 10), whose physiognomy of shame is made up of infant bodies. Through a process of "miniaturization," the rhetorical trope has scaled a historical event down to a single image; the very concept of mimesis has been turned on its head, so to speak.[10] Ironically, the vermiculate presence of the innocent victims heightens their deadness at the hand of the one who led them to a common tragedy. In a way, metonymy has outdone itself, since the visual metaphor has made it possible for individual parts to radiate a cluster of meanings ranging from guilt and shame to murder. From pictorial arrangement to literary tropes involving adjunction, suppression, substitution, permutation, extension, restriction, and displacement, technique falls back on the rhetorical *mise en miniature* of what Gilbert Durant calls the euphemistic space of the fantastic, which was so very familiar to mannerist goldsmiths and art collectors.[11] Often mimesis was scaled down to a reductive concept that favored fragmentation and intensification.

IV

In Comanini's words, mannerist *capricci* brought to the fore forms that "do not exist outside the mind—*cose che non hanno l'essere fuor della mente.*" Set as Arcimboldo was against any direct mimesis of nature, Flora and Vertumnus were painted by

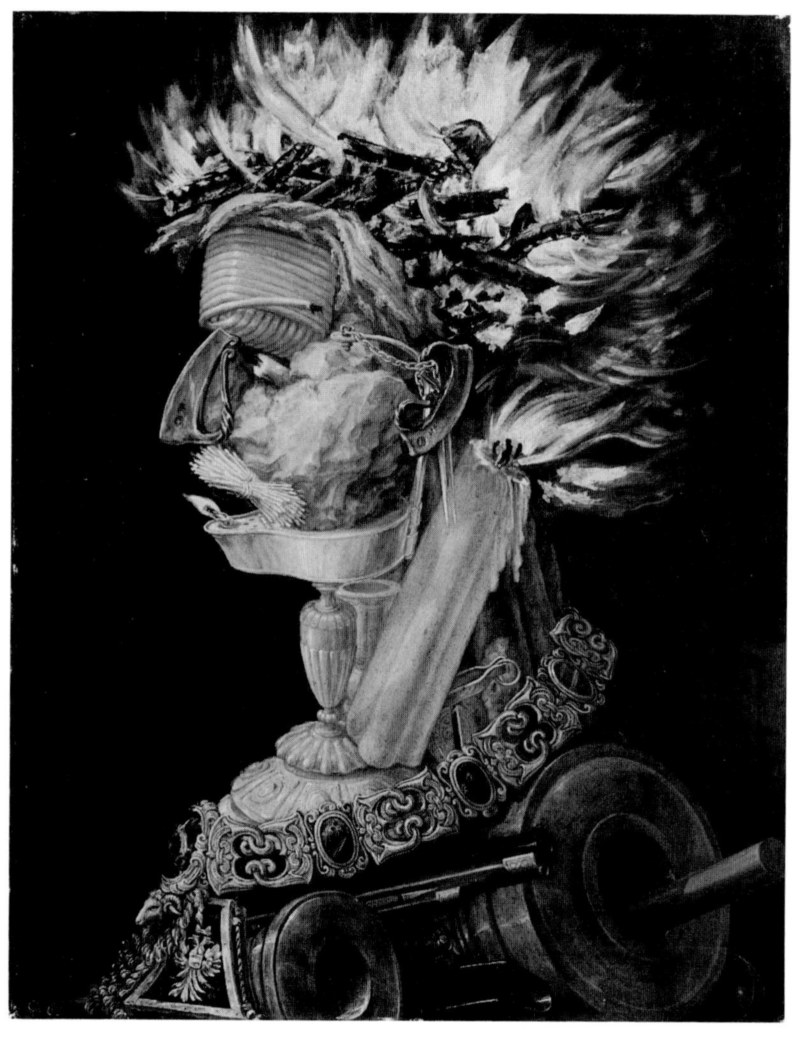

Fig. 9. Giuseppe Arcimboldo, *The Fire,* 1566. Kunsthistorisches Museum, Vienna

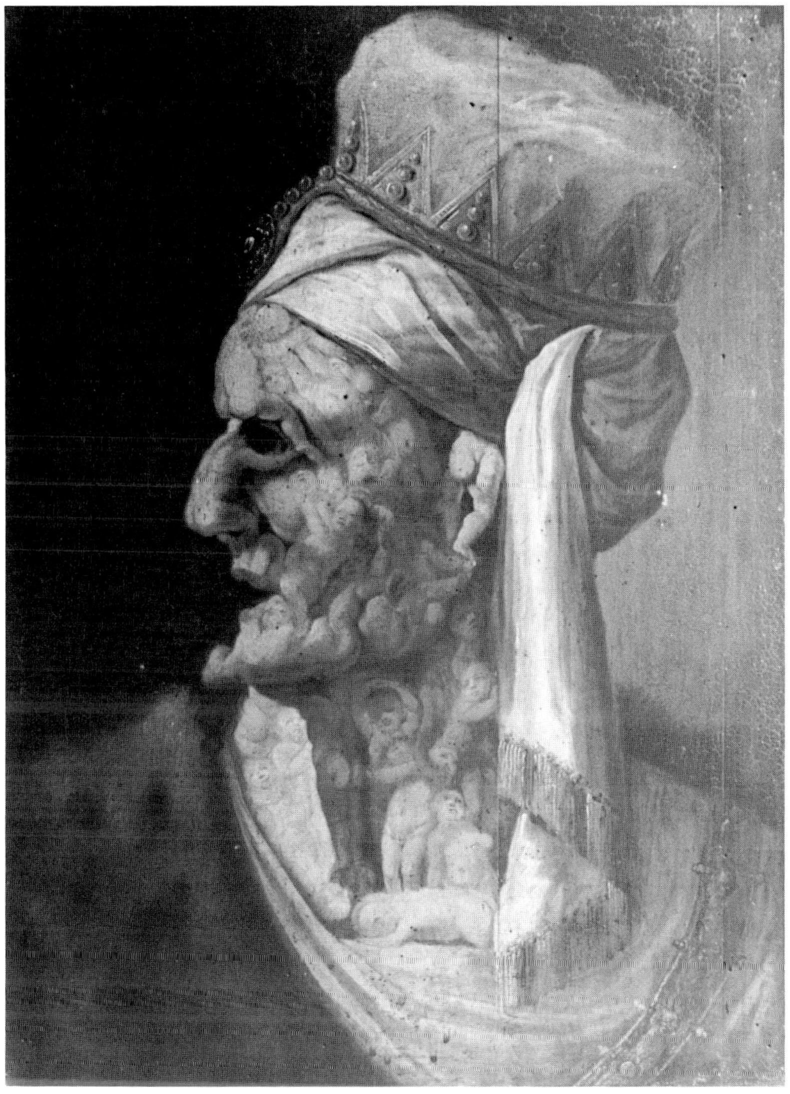

Fig. 10. Giuseppe Arcimboldo, *Herod's Head*, 1566? Tiroler Landesmuseum Ferdinandeum, Innsbruck

an "*ingegnosissimo pittore fantastico*" (*Trattati,* 3:257). Because it favored invention over imitation, fantasy often steered originality toward the excessive mode of the grotesque. By the early sixteenth century, Michael Levey writes, "*invenzione* was consciously challenging nature, and art was to be that which went beyond imitation."[12] Benedetto Varchi drew a line between substantial and contingent forms. The first are mimetic, whereas the latter's origin "is not in the things that are made, but in him who makes them."[13] Because it exceeds the uniformity of nature, contingency falls back on fantasy, which Martin Kemp describes as an "active, combinatory imagination—which continually recombines sensory impressions, visualizing new compounds in unending abundance."[14] Emulation yielded *capricci, ghiribizzi,* and *grottesche* that flaunted artificiality through an unending array of grotesque guises.

A number of Arcimboldo's drawings (*Agriculture, Kitchen*) and paintings (*Cook, Fire*) followed in the rich tradition of *apparati* and *automi.*[15] Artificiality thus operated in an anticlassical free zone where the grotesque edged on the turf of experimental sciences.[16] From the seemingly organic to the apparently mechanical, Arcimboldo's figures retain an overwhelming emphasis on details. His "technological" portrait of *The Librarian* (Fig. 11) could be set at the start of a line including the *Cubist Designs* (1590s) of Cambiaso and Bracelli's tennis players made out of tennis rackets (*Capricci,* 1624). Surviving those who write books and build civilizations, the librarian is an indestructable symbol of the emergent proliferation of books. Rather than depicting artists at work in the baroque mode of creative activity (Cervantes, Velázquez), Arcimboldo chose to replace "creative writing" with the collection of books—inventory instead of invention.

The Librarian is literally made up of books. As a trope whereby parts stand for the whole, synecdoche is so abundant that it seems to claim the contextuality of a collection. The book stands for the librarian as well as for the library. At first the anthropomorphic guise—or disguise—seems to mix old and new by flaunting elegant bookmarkers that verge on a "miniaturization" of chivalric banners. Inside, the figure affords no ego

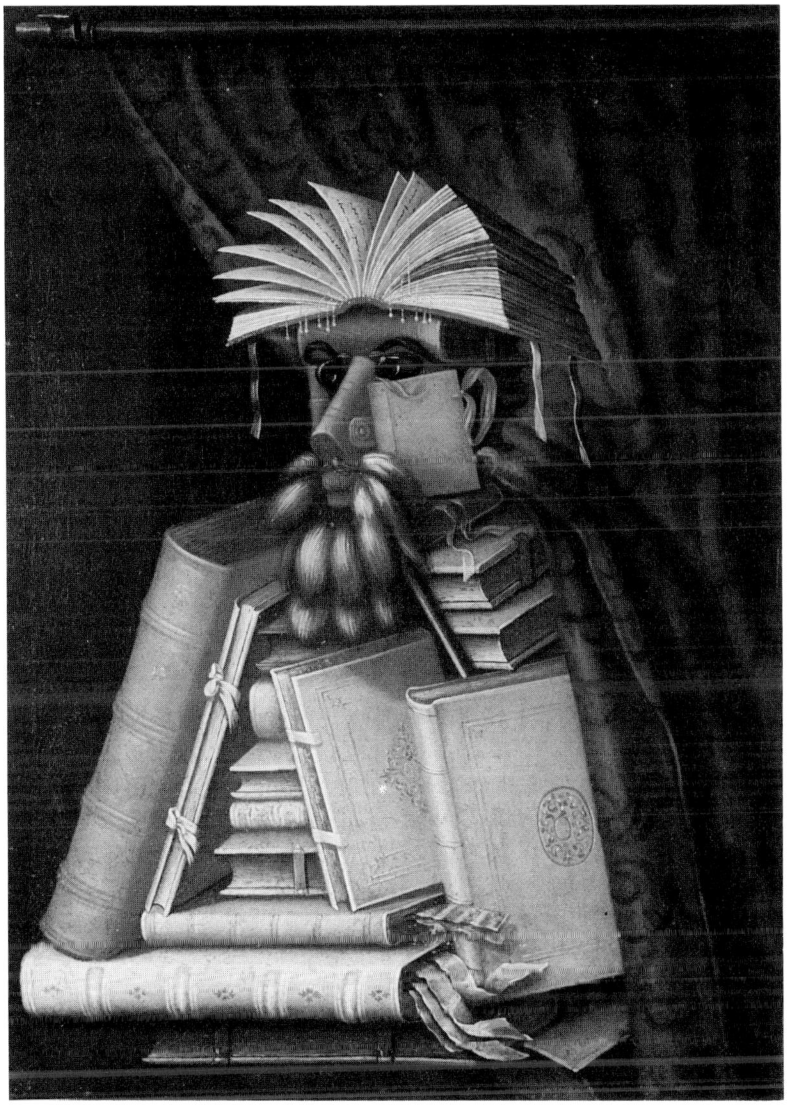

Fig. 11. Giuseppe Arcimboldo, *The Librarian*. Skoklosters Slott, Stockholm

that might claim either professional or intellectual stature. The anonymous tomes set up the book as an object whose many bookmarks signal usage but fail to identify authors and titles.

Throughout the fifteenth century, Jerome, Augustine, and Federigo da Montefeltro were presented as scholars and leaders by Botticelli, Carpaccio, Antonello da Messina, and Pedro Berruguete. The *Cinquecento,* instead, began to foreground libraries and books (Arcimboldo, Doni).[17] The qualitative became quantitative. At a time when the printing press was on its way to give universal range to the availability of knowledge, books multiplied in the privacy of homes. A tender care guides the fingers of sixteenth-century ladies through Petrarchan tomes that preserve manuscript traces of the original hand in Andrea del Sarto's *Portrait of a Girl Holding a Volume of Petrarch* and in *Portrait of Laura Battiferri* by Bronzino.[18] By contrast, a poem written by Bettino da Trizzo praised the new way—"*nuovo modo*"—of making books in abundance—"*far libri in abondantia.*" Somehow, quantifications of that sort had to affect artistic output; and it is fair to suggest that mannerist *maniere* met the challenge; the Arcimboldesque and the Petrarchan carried the day. In a rather short time, the very bulk of printed materials made it possible for books to circulate within a world of their own. Abundance, if not excess, influenced production and reception alike.

From Cervantes and Velázquez to Vermeer, baroque artists were interested in the creative activity of pens and paintbrushes, whereas the tomelike makeup of *The Librarian* proved that the *studiolo* was not so much a place of intellectual growth as a room where books were stored. Even though he stands where the instruments of learning are gathered, the librarian neither takes in nor acts out knowledge. Without a name, he exists as the shell-like form of a professional "it-id." Cunningly, matters of technology have overpowered learning, knowledge, and ideology.

From *studiolos* to *Wunderkammern,* artists focused on spaces where the co-presence of heterogeneous forms cut into the integrity of time, genre, and representation. It is less than a curiosity to remind ourselves that Arcimboldo spent most of his productive years (1562–87) at the court of Rudolph II, whose *Wunder-*

kammer—much like Bertonius's *Raritätenkabinett* and Duke Ferdinand of Tirol's *grosse Kunstkammer*—were meant to house the bizarre and the *un*natural. South of the Alps, the *studiolo* of Francesco I in Florence (Palazzo Vecchio) was to serve as a closet of rare and precious things. It was Arcimboldo's duty to purchase antiquities, art objects, and exotic animals for patrons who cherished Roman *curiosa artificialia.* Less than coincidentally, Athenasius Kircher also owned a *Wunderkammer,* and his puzzle-picture *Campus anthropomorphus* (1646) updated Arcimboldo's landscape heads.

Such artificial places drew into the cumulative landscape of an encyclopedic memory all that history and geography had dispersed throughout time and space. The very act of "museumfying" fixed into immobility an array of objects set next to other objects.[19] Their contiguity was indeed akin to the tassels that make up Arcimboldo's portraits. In both cases, art fell back on a disjunctive vocabulary capable of giving an unprecedented sense of togetherness—if not belonging—to what had always been there.[20] Toward the end of the sixteenth century, cultural taste on both sides of the Alps tested the range of the marvelous, and formal concerns often took on a life of their own.

V

Mimesis became a rhetorical device on Arcimboldo's pictorial chessboard, which flirted with transfers and transgressions. According to Ferdinand de Saussure's famous simile, language is like a game of chess, and Arcimboldo played the game with skill. For virtuosity's sake, he violated the standing grammar of painting to the point that the object masked itself, perspective betrayed form, and composition broke loose of mimesis.

Experimentation thus became crucial to a *bella maniera* that parodied the exemplary *maniera moderna* of Raphael and Michelangelo. Throughout the sixteenth century, it was fashionable to add the suffix *-esco* to masters who set vogues. Stressing the adjectival rather than the nominal guise, the nomenclature of art was studded with neologisms: *raffaellesco, leonardesco,* and *bernesco.* Successful *maniere* muted concerns with subject matter into stylistic variations known as *ghiribizzi, capricci,* and *bizzarrie.*

Instead of enhancing the unity of ideas, *ut pictura poesis* turned into a mechanism of formal transfers across the arts. Like other mannerists, Arcimboldo fabricated one art out of the materials of another.[21] With time, the very success of such inventions (*capricci*) hardened into clichés. The outcome, Jean Cohen would warn us, is typical of artforms thriving on rhetorical figures; inevitably "*la poétique structurale*" raises "*le spectre redoutable de la machine, de la production automatique.*"[22] Consensus somehow disciplined excess.

Language was a battleground for such exchanges, and Arcimboldo seems to have taken pleasure in toying with its semantics. Rhetoric took precedence over meaning, and the vocabulary of painting became tautological. Literature followed suit. Ugo Scoti-Bertinelli has called attention to the "mannered" verbosity of Vasari's language,[23] which was replete with expressions such as *varia diversità, discordante concordia, disgraziatissima grazia, havuto s'avesse,* or *avuto non avevano.* And Anton Francesco Doni wrote in *La libraria* (1557)[24] that many books are nothing more than wheels mixing words with other words ("*ruota di parole*") over and over again ("*rimescolando parole con parole.*" Redundancy became self-fulfilling once language proved to be both deviant and devious. It deviated from its "origin" in reality, and its concealed duplicity undermined the assurance with which it is commonly used.[25]

In his discussion of the *poema eroico* (1562–64), Tasso defended Aristotle's *Rhetoric* against widespread abuses. Although critical of *istrioni* and histrionics, he praised literary *artifici.* His eccentric usage of language was congruous with that of perspective. While excellence of style rested with "oblique or distorted poetic expression—*parlare obliquo o distorto,*" the "doubling of words" was an "ornament crucial to poetry—*duplicare le parole ancora è ornamento ch'arricchisce e fa magnifica la poesia.*" Repetition ("*replicare*") could come at the beginning or in the middle of the line, and "the double voice" particularly enriched expression—"*particolarmente gonfia il parlare la voce raddoppiata.*"[26] Indeed, we confront a literary counterpart to the multiple grammar of Arcimboldo's visual language, which also made a case for Hocke's concept of "perspectivism."

By definition, *ghiribizzi* refer to that which does not exist, and it was believed that they stemmed from minds bent to seek "what they do not have."[27] In terms of generic transgressions, *capricci* and *ghiribizzi* point to variations on a theme or from the normal, anticonventional attitudes, the opposite of truth or nature, or even a sketch. With time, technique so affected genre that Francesco Patrizi linked it to emotional categories instead of Aristotelian rules. Poetic wonderment gained consensus, which thrived on eccentricity.

Like *capriccio* and *ghiribizzo, bizzarria* touched on an associative field ranging from *fantastico* to *stravagante.* Toward the end of the sixteenth century, *bizzarro* defined a formal category when interest in such eccentric forms as *strano, contraffatto, ingegnoso, caricaturale,* and *iperbolico* flourished. Patrizi's twelve sources of the marvelous included novelty, paradox, augmentation, the unusual, the extranatural, and the unexpected. All such forms were irregular rather than revolutionary, and often fell between the generic layers that separated portraits, landscapes, "*rustici,*" and still lifes. Accordingly, Guarini mixed dramatic modes in *Il pastor fido* (1590) and the *Compendium of Tragicomic Poetry* (1599), while Mario Bettini painted anamorphic pictures and wrote a comic-satiric-pastoral tragedy, the *Hilarotragoedia Satyropastoralis.*[28]

In the preface to the Third Book of the *Lives,* perfection in art draws from both *regola* (rule) and *licenzia* (invention, antirule). Artists "still lacked, within the boundaries of the rules, a freedom which—not being part of the rules—was nevertheless ordained by the rules and which could coexist with order without causing confusion or spoiling it—*mancando ancora nella regola una licenzia che, non essendo di regola, fusse ordinata nella regola, e potesse stare senza fare confusione o guastare l'ordine.*" The weight of authorities such as Leonardo, Raphael, and Michelangelo was brought to bear on the generic dualism rule-antirule of mannerist *capricci.* Vasari did not promote absolute freedom, but freedom at the other side of norm. Comanini also believed that *sprezzatura artificiosa* would derail the symmetries of "*contraposto con contraposto*" and antithesis with antithesis. By contrast, forms without "any correspondence" (*Trattati,* 3:362) would be set against the "predictability" of both discourse and proportion. Vincenzo Danti had that goal in mind when he defined *proporzione artificiosa:* "The proportion of unequal things will be ever more artificial and will produce a greater beauty than conformity to similar things" (*Trattati,* 1:234).[29] Excess was relational, for it began where norms ended. However stupefying, the result was not unbridled originality, but a rather parasitic inventiveness suited for the mental sloth of drawing-room societies equally at ease in Fontainebleau and Rudolphine Prague.

Whether it be a portrait or a poem, the experience of surprise in front of Arcimboldesque artworks points to what Patrizi called the faculty of marveling (*potenza ammirativa*), whose very function is to exaggerate. Art deceives, and we willingly let ourselves be outwitted. Whereas linear perspective gave viewers images of cognitive unity, Arcimboldo placed them at the most oblique intersection of epistemological planes. At all times, he played with the counterfeit of reality. His penchant for bizarre permutations thrived at the surface, where his text-tableau was prone to be rhetorically unsequential and pictorially unspatial.[30]

VI

With Arcimboldo, the symbolic meaning of the perspective metaphor—to see clearly is to know with certainty—yielded to concerns with the mechanics of pictorial illusionism. *Pictura* stretched its autonomous potential to the limit. Matters of perspective ceased to be linear and became "curious." The language of metaphor followed suit. To borrow from Kenneth Burke, "metaphor is a device for seeing something *in terms* of something else. It brings out the thisness of a that, and the thatness of a this."[31] Excess became methodological; technique measured the out-of-sight, courted the unproportional, and fed on virtuosity.

Because he was more interested in details than in the contexuality of humanist *istorie,* Arcimboldo focused on the basic units of rhetoric. Cicero provided the blueprint for such exercises when he separated "extrinsic" from "intrinsic" topics. The first depend on outside authority, whereas the second are inherent to the subject in the guise of definition, enumeration of parts, cognate words, contradictions, and comparisons with important events. In visual terms, "intrinsic" topics of that kind correspond to Arcimboldo's titles, his lists-additions of animals-flowers-utensils, fire-firearms, and head-Herod-history. Beyond Ciceronian hopes of setting philosophy and rhetoric at pace, the latter often took the lead in the sixteenth century.[32]

To the extent that it reconstructs the external world, the Albertian concept of perspective is a "cognitive metaphor."[33] Alberti set sight and knowledge on equal footing because he believed in the visual clarity of intellectual certainty. That axiom was central to the symbolism of linear perspective. In the world of art, gestures enacted a code of literary-philosophical signs, and the rhetorical pictorialism of the *istoria* was declared to be the most important part of painting. Perspective, history, and mimesis were but aspects of the representational grammar of knowledge. Art perpetuated the belief that language lies buried in representational realism. Humanist space in fact was a discursive space.

As the sixteenth century unfolded, Parmigianino's *Self-portrait in a Convex Mirror* (Fig. 12), Vignola's anamorphoses (*Le due regole della prospettiva,* 1583), and the treatises of Daniello Barbaro and Paolo Lomazzo subverted the uses perspective was meant to serve. If turned upside down, Arcimboldo's *The Cook* and *The Man and the Vegetables* (see Fig. 2) can become dishes of vegetables and roasted meat. Just as paradox turns language against itself by asserting both terms of a contradiction at once, so did the artist turn perspective and mimesis against each other. It was a time when the macaronic Muse of Gastronomy fed pasta and polenta to ludic bards. One of them was Teofilo Folengo, whose mock-epic *Baldus* (1517) parodied in macaronic Latin Ariosto's *poema cavalleresco.* Roland Barthes would suggest that such a cluster of works foregrounds the interplay between denota-

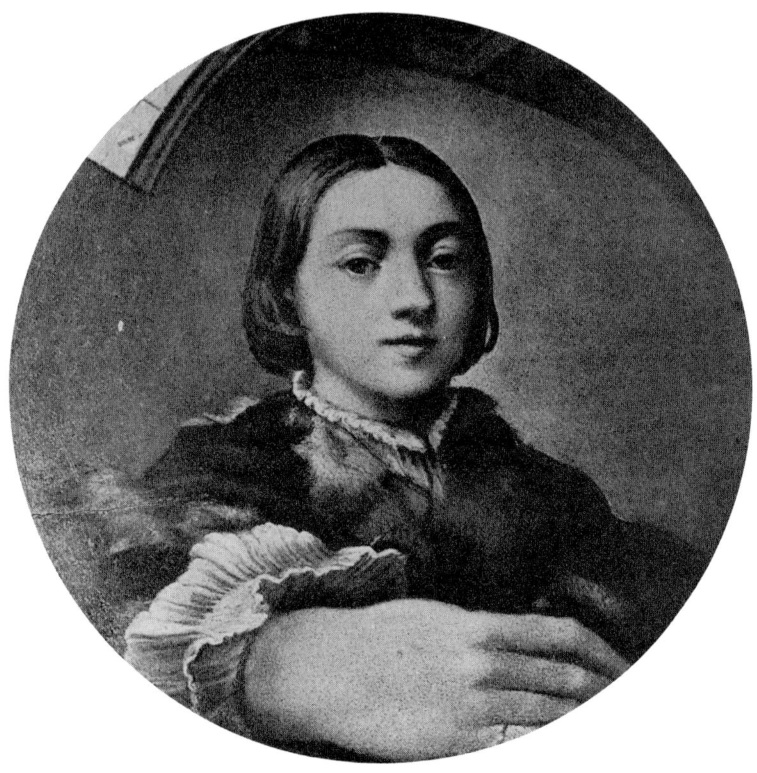

Fig. 12. Parmigianino, *Self-Portrait in a Convex Mirror,* 1524. Kunsthistorisches Museum, Vienna

tion and connotation, which "enables the text to operate like a game, each system referring to the other according to the requirements of a certain *illusion*."[34]

Arcimboldo stopped short of macaronic realism in his *Genius of Cooking* (*Cucina*, 1569; Fig. 13), which presented the technology of eating through a portrait made up with culinary utensils. Against Rabelaisian delights in edible products ready for consumption, gastronomy was reduced to an array of metal gadgets and silver plates. Meaning itself followed suit in a sonnet pinned to the print:

> Che miri o sciocco questa mia pittura
> Di tanti al viver nostro atti stromenti,
> E fai nel tuo pensier vari argomenti,
> Immagine non è, non è figura.
> . . . .
> Quindi Natura a l'Arte adombrar parmi,
> Che per bisogno si fe' a l'arte amica,
> Lungi dal suo costume antico, et empio.
>
> (Confused viewer, you who admire my painting
> Of many instruments useful to your living,
> And develop numerous arguments in your mind,
> It is not an image, it is not a figure.
> It thus seems to me that Nature adumbrates Art;
> Having felt the need of befriending art
> Nature abandoned its ancient and unworthy practice.)

The first stanza sets up a doubt that twice denies identity to the subject, which is neither an image nor a figure. Links between literal details and the symbolic whole are at least bizarre. Since the verb *parmi* weighs on opinion rather than fact, the viewer's search for "mimetic" explanations is stalled in the last tercet. Although one would expect the preposition "therefore" to forward a logical sequence, meaning comes to an impasse at the end of the line. Actually the reverse has taken place; the mimetic has befriended the fantastic. Viewers are expected to test the ancient habit of measuring art against the forms of reality.

Once the ideological framework of humanist imperatives began to falter during the sixteenth century, arrangement began to claim precedence over invention. For novelty's sake, patterns of order made room for irregularities that enhanced style and teased subject matter. Without exceeding the boundaries of his

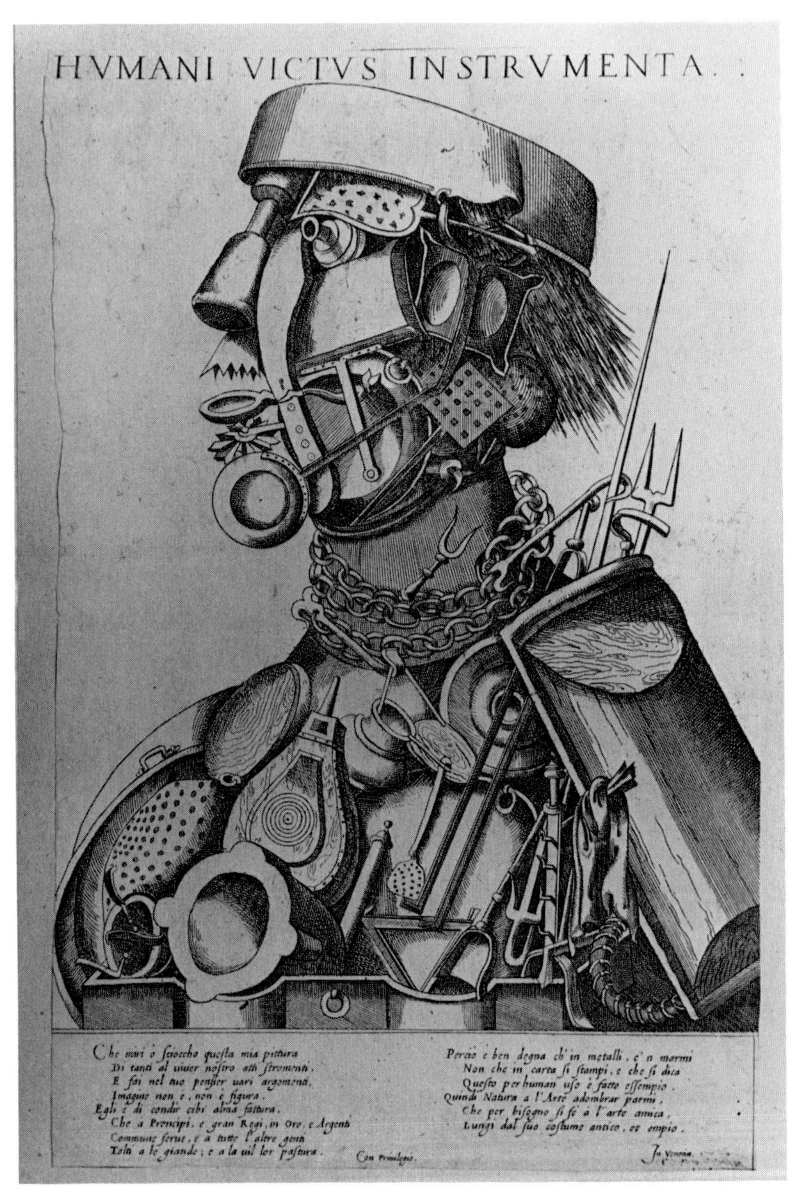

Fig. 13. Giuseppe Arcimboldo, *The Genius of Cooking*, 1569. Museum of Decorative Arts, Copenhagen

portraits, Arcimboldo parodied *ars, ingenium,* and mimesis. At the peak of contemporary debates on Aristotelian "credible impossibles" and "incredible possibles," originality brought out unmimetic images.

The "meaning" of artistic forms no longer was to be taken as a matter of truth. Later, Nietzsche raised a fundamental question that shed a retrospective light:

> What therefore is truth? A mobile army of metaphors, metonymies, anthropomorphisms: in short, a sum of human relations which became potentially and rhetorically intensified, metamorphosed, adorned, and after long usage seem to a nation fixed, canonic and binding; truths are illusions of which one has forgotten that they *are* illusions.[35]

Arcimboldo is there to remind us that illusions are only illusions. Because he commandeered the army of linguistic eccentricities better than most, his art flaunts "appearance," which foregrounds its own epistemological unreliability.

In a fundamental sense, the painter tied rhetoric and perspective to style. As signs of the times, Arcimboldo's portraits suggest that painting does not imitate reality but rather a representation of it—indeed, the representation of a representation. His deliberate category mistake tested the untapped potential of literary and pictorial transgressions. In his canvases, I would suggest, perspective proved to be a rhetorical rather than a cognitive metaphor.

VII

At the beginning of the sixteenth century, *The Courtier* of Castiglione and Raphael's frescoes in the Stanza della Segnatura raised humanist idealism to a point where the Aristotelian-Platonic edifice was so perfectly ordered that there was very little one could add to it, except ornament and decorative idealism.

Voicing a general attitude, Tasso later wrote: "If it is true that decoration makes things that are not beautiful appear to be so, the result will not be the beautiful, but a travesty of it. Beauty makes things beautiful, whereas decoration only makes them appear to be so. Therefore, the difference between decoration and beauty is like that between true and false, reality and appearance."[36] Hedonistic approaches to art stood out. While it does not teach, ornament makes surfaces attractive; moreover, it can alter imitation to the point that even "the beautiful is transmutable, and like the chameleon takes on different colors, different forms and diverse appearances." Originality nurtured extravagance, and Arcimboldo was one of many artists who believed that there was no longer any virtue in simple statements, since there were no simple certainties to state. As it happened, even eccentricity became predictable when *ghiribizzi* proved to be "typically" irregular. Like ornament, the eccentric style did not teach. Actually it did not even pretend to, since it aimed only at ludic entertainment.

The notion that man is the ideal measure of all things was a cornerstone of classical and humanist art. For Arcimboldo, man measured everything in the sense that his form contained all things. Since no other measure could be found, anthropomorphism still set cosmos apart from chaos. Nevertheless, "everything" became predominant. The human outline lodged an addable multitude of objects in much the same way as the *Wunderkammer* and *Raritätenkabinett* treasured a wealth of things.[37] The measure had been lost, and the world of things was about to overflow in all directions. To maintain some sense of order, knowledge often was reduced to an inventory of reality that was stored in the only frame of order: the canvas itself. Form became catalogue, which could present unusual things without having to interpret them.

In Arcimboldo's art, man is not an idea but a shape, and a grotesque one at that. As an anatomical vessel, the body could take in a heap of objects. "The great man of the Renaissance," Erwin Panofsky writes, "asserted his personality centripetally, so to speak: he swallowed up the world that surrounded him until his whole environment had been absorbed by his own self."[38] Keeping Arcimboldo's superficiality in mind, I would guess that his figures did not swallow the world. Instead, the world got stuck in their throats, and they had to regurgitate it all over their bodies. Because they could neither exist in space nor function as living forms, those figures could not swallow at all. Actually they could link up to reality only by housing it within their own body, which became a kind of treasure chest in which things could replace other things endlessly.

Mannerist intake and outtake proved to be equally gargantuan. In light of the old saying, man is a little world, and everything can be stored in that world. So conceived, art needed only to make the icastic presence of things attractive. At the other side of imitation, mannerist eccentricity courted a metaphorical *altérité* that fell beyond the discipline of mimetic standards.

VIII

Tensions between mimetic and fantastic modes of expression became critical toward the end of the *Cinquecento*. As a spokesman for the *Controriforma*, Cardinal Paleotti censured painters of *grottesche*, who indulged in "appearances . . . painting things which are not true" (*Trattati*, 2:452). Conversely, appearance was crucial to Arcimboldo. Things neither live nor die in his canvases, since time and vitality never entered his bloodless mosaics. Taking on a life of its own, artificiality defied vision, perception, and knowledge itself.

For representation's sake, Arcimboldo "simulated" the image of man, and "dissimulated" a world of things. He was one of many artists who set out to say things abnormally rather than normally, letting affectation prevail over spontaneity. As proud as a peacock of his own performance, Arcimboldo dazzled the world of art with an extravagant panegyric to artifice.[39]

3

Adumbration of Nature and the Liminality of Pictorial Delight

Si trattava di un manierismo tutto esteriore, tutto risolto in una illuminazione a freddo della scorza linguistica, per cui la "locuzione" doveva valere appunto come involucro, quasi annullando le tracce di quanto una volta sotto l'involucro doveva pur essere stato presente. Un manierismo che in effetti non aveva molti spazi di manovra, che doveva finire per isolarsi in una ripetitività di se stesso.

—Giulio Ferroni

I

Just as Alberti's treatise on painting drew from the experience of earlier artists, so did Comanini's *Il Figino overo del fine della pittura* lean back on Ariosto, Tasso, Giulio Romano, and Arcimboldo. In a kind of closed circuit, artists inspired critics who wrote for well-trained practitioners. Because it followed the practice and sealed the success of excellent artists, much theoretical writing was predicated on the superlative. Emulation therefore started at the top; since it could not go up, it had to turn sideways. And it did.

During the second half of the *Cinquecento,* a harvest of writings on theory and criticism affected tragedy, the epic, and *ut pictura poesis* in excess of what Horace and Aristotle had ever dared. At times, revivals of the past could develop strange mixtures of reverence and defiance. Baxter Hathaway reminds us that criticism took up divided concerns with life as against "the age-old demand for the marvelous in myth and poetry—the escaping from this world of brass into a golden one of fantasy."[1] Adumbrations of nature gained strength in the practice of the arts, and eccentricity explored bizarre regions of artistic invention.

Within sight of the age-old demand for the marvelous, this chapter takes up sections of Comanini's treatise that shed light on the liminal province of mannerist *delectare.* Because it wavered between "making" likenesses and "making up" artifice, excellence came to depend on taste, style, and caprice.[2] Art was to outdo—not to imitate—nature.

II

Having given the Platonic tradition of the dialogue form a parodic slant, Comanini had the theologian Martinengo and the poet Guazzo visit Figino, a sick painter who asks them to read a poem that the author himself had sent him. The ensuing debate on the nature of genius centers on illness, which has halted the practice of painting:

> Sta 'l pennello in disparte,
> Onde imitar solea
> Così 'l vero col finto,
> Che 'l ver rimanea vinto
> Dal falso, che del ver più ver parea;
> Tal ch'ombre i frutti e i fiori
> Eran di quei ch'ombraro i suoi colori.

(Now the paintbrush lies idle,
Which once used to imitate
Reality as well as fiction
To the point where reality was conquered
By fiction, which appeared to be more real than the real;
So that fruits and flowers were but shadows
Of those fruits and flowers
Adumbrated by his colors.)

From a mimetic standpoint, artifice is more impressive than reality, which can be only a shallow copy of art. The key word is fiction ("*falso-finto*"), which was to be set within a mimetic range that would allow the forms of art to emerge from the shadows of nature—"*ombre i frutti e i fiori.*" Comanini's choice of verbs such as "*parea*" and "*ombraro*"—to seem and to adumbrate—are Arcimboldo's own; both set art in a realm of intentional ambiguity.

By combining the icastic with the fantastic, the artwork took the reality of things as a point of departure, a matter to be fictionalized into "*credible maraviglioso*" (*Trattati,* 3:354–55). By the same token, the beautiful work of art had to be "natural and artificial—*naturale et artificioso*" (254); as such, it stemmed from an eccentric mixture that courted parodic *dis*junctions more than analogical *con*junctions. The painter began to look at pictorial fictions as "sources" for emulating nature, which had been paved over by the artistic tradition. The standard of art was art itself: "*Che del ver più ver parea.*"

In the guise of fantastic shapes, mimesis of the artistic tradition offered a way out of gregarious modes "in the manner of." At the turn of the seventeenth century, Tesauro would have admired Arcimboldo for having written a verse that combined two negatives: "*Immagine non è, non è figura.*"[3] In *The Genius of Cooking* (see Fig. 13), canvas and poem present neither the imitation of a known likeness nor the representation of a human figure, but a mixture of both: a figure of speech. Art was not ground-breaking but self complacent. Because of its popularity, "outdoing" nature and tradition alike became normative rather than transgressive. G. A. Gilio empowered art to "make what nature cannot" ("*arte facendo quello che la natura non può per se stessa fare*"; *Trattati,* 1:100–117).[4]

III

In the realm of marvels, ideology made room for playfulness, and even myth bore a mannerist guise in Comanini's approach to it:

Fresco rivo in bel prato
Finse dentro il pensiero
Il buon Pittore, per poi ritrarlo un giorno.
Or, mentre è più lassato,
Finge anco un sasso intero,
. . . .
Al fier Tantalo l'onda
Scherza intorno la bocca;
Ma fugge, se vuol berla, et ei bee sabbia.

(A fresh river in a beautiful meadow
Imagined in his mind
The good Painter, who would some day paint it.
Now, while he is more relaxed
he imagines an enormous rock
. . . .
Waves play by the mouth
of the proud Tantalus;
but they retreat when he reaches for them, and he drinks sand.)

Nature plays—"*scherza*"—with man, and Tantalus accepts the deceit. In its mythic disguise, extravagance gained strength from its own lightheartedness. Comanini's verbal nomenclature of *fingere, scherzare,* and *ombrare* favored a sportive approach to art. In fact, "all imitative arts find in pleasure their proper and adequate goal. Since painting is one of these arts, it is proper to say that pleasure, and not the useful, constitutes its goal" (*Trattati,* 3:248). Didacticism waned, and eccentricity became a predominant measure of excellence at the hedonistic periphery of art.

Since he created *credibile maraviglioso,* Comanini's *artifex* would qualify as a *homo ludens* exceedingly partial to the pleasurable. Because it stands at bay of experience, ludic activity takes place in an artificial sphere extraneous to any "ordinary" life: "If painting is imitation, it is game; and imitation always involves pleasure; and pleasure is the goal of play; it therefore follows that pleasure is the proper goal of painting" (*Trattati,* 3:285). Comanini and Arcimboldo therefore shifted the Latin meaning of *ludus* as military, educational, or athletic training to autonomy in the practice of art.[5] On the playground of the mind, their riddlelike forms aimed at breaking customary responses for unusual results. Personification itself became a game, and they made it their own on literary and pictorial chessboards that have bewildered viewers ever since.

Already at the turn of the sixteenth century, Michael Levey writes, it was not uncommon for the artist to withdraw from conventions and play up eccentricity.[6] Arcimboldo's puzzle portraits therefore followed in the mainstream of artworks that were meant to be pleasantly superfluous. In *Récepte véritable* (1563), Bernard Palissy harnessed imagination and technology for his project of a statue with a book in one hand and a vase in the other. Anyone stepping forward to read would experience firsthand whatever the vase would empty out on him. The humanist ritual of reading books in the *studiolo* became ludic outdoors; the "source" turned into a gamely "bait." Within the Italian tradition, it suffices to mention the "wetting sports" at Bagnaia and Villa d'Este in Tivoli near Rome, Giambologna's *Appennino* at Pratolino (see Fig. 7), and the collapsing Sala dei Giganti by Giulio Romano (see Fig. 6), who oppressed viewers with a kind of environmental derangement. To borrow from Comanini's comments on the frescoes, "*diletto*" dispensed viewers from moral concerns with the tragic downfall of the giants.

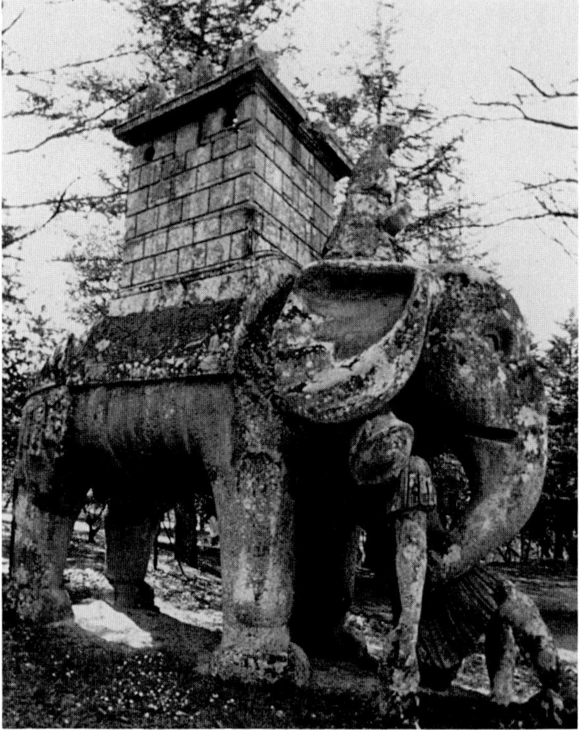

Fig. 14. Bosco sacro, Bomarzo

Horror and compassion were disregarded because of a ludic presumption that preempted preoccupations with truths hidden below the surface. People were to approach the artwork lethetically; their disbelief in those outrageous scenes presumed that those images were independent of the real world.[7]

Outdoors, Vicino Orsini's monsters in the fantastic *bosco* at Bomarzo (Figs. 14, 15) stupefied visitors through shifts in perspective, incredible apparitions, contrasts of light and darkness, houses with inclined pavements and walls off center that tested spatial standards beyond plausibility. Just as viewers are confused by Arcimboldo's figure, so are they disoriented by the

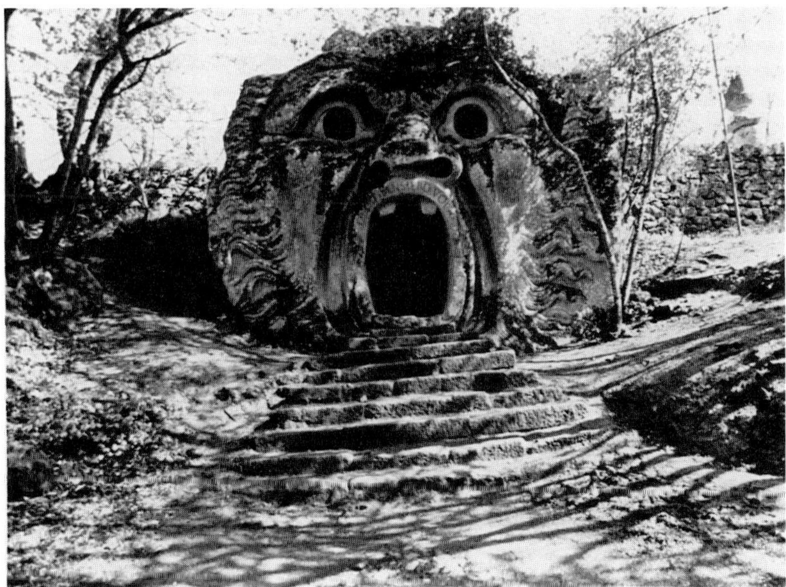

Fig. 15. Bosco sacro, Bomarzo

inscription in the tilted house: "Tell me if such marvelous things have been made by deceit or by art."[8] Once uncertainty became self-fulfilling, the conditional ("if") touched off a mode of expression whereby double sense obscured meaning.

Centuries later, Manuel Mujica-Lainez so fictionalized Vicino Orsini's plan for the Sacred Wood: "I did not want, for nothing would have been more contrary to my imaginative originality, for the woods at Bomarzo to be transformed into a symmetrical park of exact logic, where every piece of construction would respond to calculated correspondences and balances. . . . What there would be of harmonious rigor in it would only serve to stress its fantasy."[9] In the world of make-believe, art badgered the literal and the conceptual alike. Correspondences between the two paved the way for unpredictable asymmetries that favored extravagance.[10]

IV

In a classical and humanist sense, "action" yielded ameliorative images of life that proved to be incompatible with icastic and fantastic standards based on life as is or as it cannot be. For Comanini, didacticism in art had to imply an operative reality, whereas pleasure warranted discontinuity. Hence, icastic—"*icastica*"—imitation deals with "things that exist in nature," while its fantastic—"*fantastica*"—counterpart invents—"*finge*"—"things that exist only in the mind of the artist." The painter who "imitates things formed by nature, such as men, animals, mountains, sea, and lands will produce an icastic imitation; but the painter who paints his own caprice (*capriccio*) never painted by anybody else, will produce a fantastic imitation" (*Trattati,* 3:274, 256). One "resembles" through perception of the external world, while the other leads representation toward the artifice of internal images.

It is on the subject of artificiality that Comanini calls on Arcimboldo to illustrate *imitazione fantastica:*

> The fantastic virtue—the function of which is to receive images transmitted by external perceptions to common sense, and to retain them, and also to compose them together—is highly developed in Arcimboldo, who, by combining the images of things seen by him, forms strange caprices that are invented by the power of imagination. That which seems impossible to combine, he unites with great dexterity, making all that he wants—*quello che pare impossibile a congiungersi accozzando con molta destrezza e facendone risultar ciò che vuole.* (*Trattati,* 3:270)

The fantastic virtue can arrange forms at will.

In the autonomous universe of art, the Arcimboldesque *Flora* (Fig. 16) gained universal praise. The iconography of Flora included the goddess and the courtesan (*Flora Meretrix*). After the middle of the sixteenth century, we find Flora surrounded by flower pots, vases, and plants of all kinds. An artist of the School of Fontainebleau, known as the "Maître de Flore," owes his name to a painting in which Flora, naked except for flowers in her lap and around her lips, sits on the ground with one arm resting on a basket filled with flowers.[11] Although associations between "name" (Flora) and "thing" (flowers) had been extensive, only Arcimboldo and his followers succeeded in making a figure of unprecedented extravagance: "a woman made of flowers" (*Trattati,* 3:257).

Mannerist ingenuity expanded the world of natural forms by transgressing nature's own orders. Often, originality called for odd treatments of what the artistic tradition had to offer. With an eye to "precedents" for mannerist *artificiosità,* the works of Piero di Cosimo could easily be singled out. His epitaph (1521) was programmatic:

> If I was strange, and strange were my figures,
> Such strangeness is a source both of grace and of art;
> And whoever adds strangeness here and there to his style,
> Gives life, force and spirit to his paintings.[12]

Vasari's presentation of his life is nothing less than the bizarre biography of a youth who enfolded originality—"*stravagante invenzione*"—into an animal-like life-style—"*uomo piuttosto bestiale che umano.*" And while others acted out the discourse of knowledge, his imagination fell prey to eccentricity.

V

Within the professional praxis of Mannerism, much art thrived on ambivalence. That mode of expression stretched the dynamics of eccentricity back and forth between ludic exaggeration and teleological resolve. Since it evaded commitments to either ideology or narrativity, the production of art suspended meaning but did not deny expression. And Comanini made ambiguity central to his own poem on the Arcimboldesque painting of *Flora* that has survived in a number of questionable versions with various titles (Figs. 17, 18):[13]

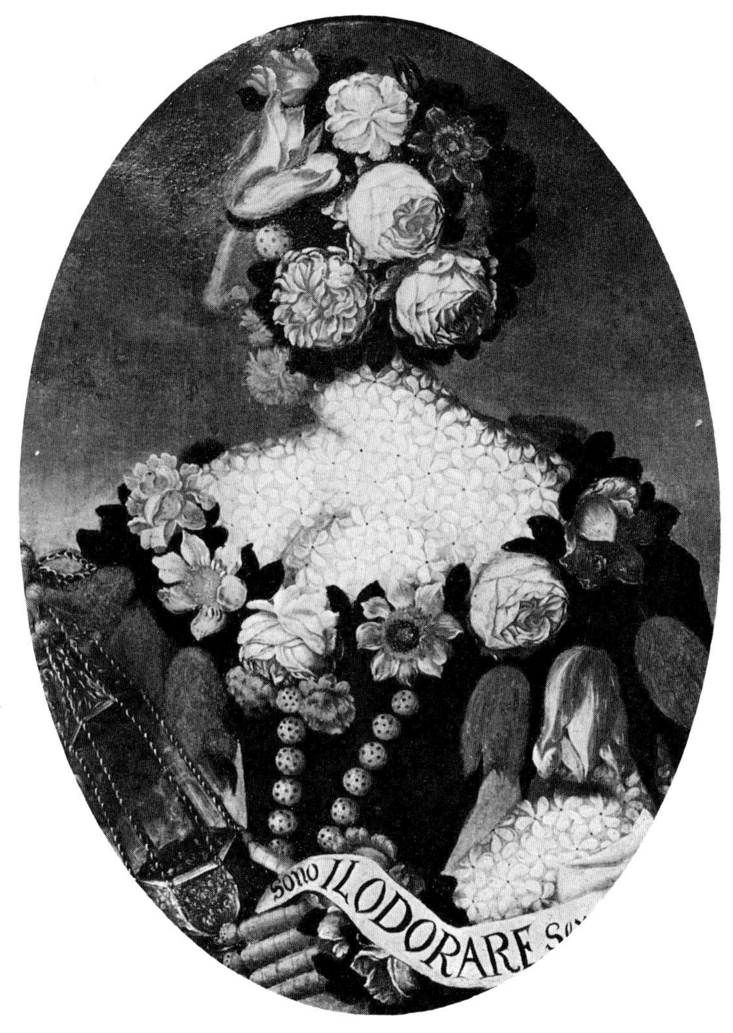

Fig. 16. Arcimboldesque School, *Flora*. Photographie Giraudon, Collection Viot, Paris

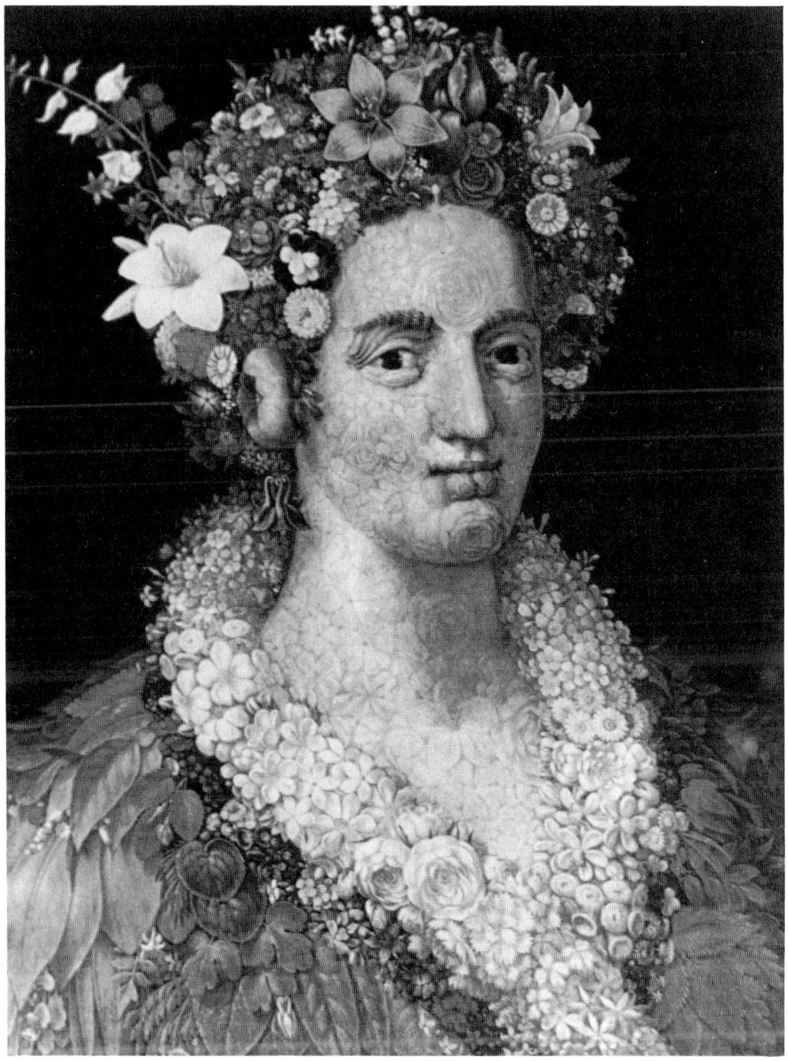

Fig. 17. Giuseppe Arcimboldo, *Flora* (?), c. 1589. Private collection

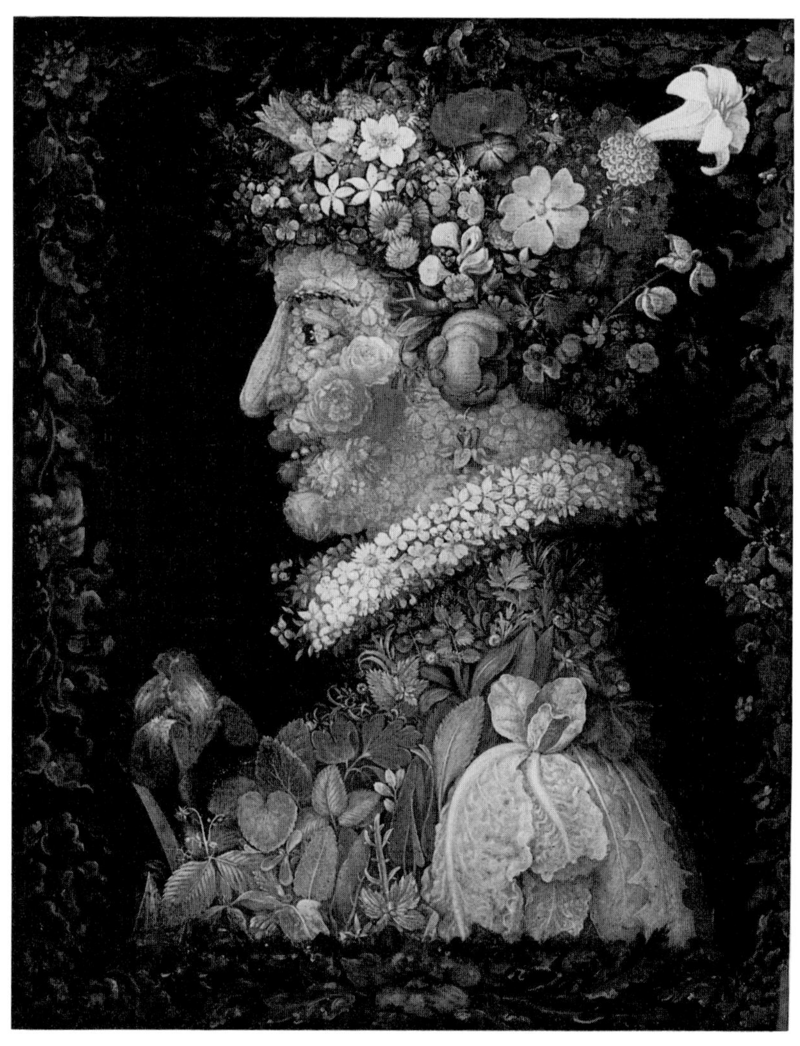

Fig. 18. Giuseppe Arcimboldo, *Spring,* 1573. Louvre, Paris

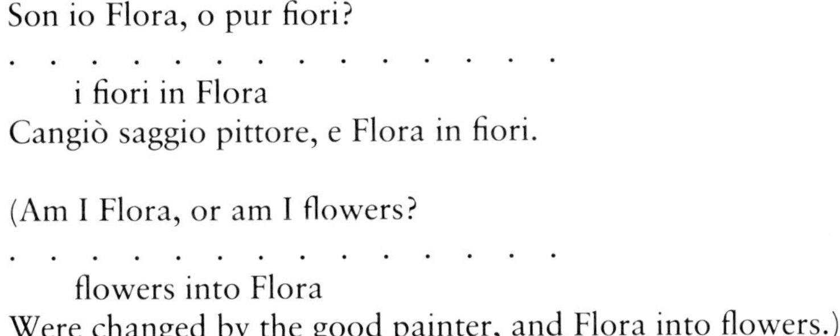

Son io Flora, o pur fiori?

. . . .

i fiori in Flora
Cangiò saggio pittore, e Flora in fiori.

(Am I Flora, or am I flowers?

. . . .

flowers into Flora
Were changed by the good painter, and Flora into flowers.)

The initial question does not expect an answer, and neither do all the others; their cumulative effect trades assertiveness for uncertainty. Question marks and hypothetical "ifs" ("se") circumvent explanation, confuse temporal sequences, and add to the spatial range of language as a technique capable of exploiting its own nomenclature to the fullest. Stemming from the resources that language offers to a kind of rhetorical soliloquy, interrogation pits that which seems to know against that which does not know. The literary text toys with inquiry and resolution alike. While the "ifs" fail to probe into any tangled reality, question marks thrive on duplicity. There is no compulsion to explain, and poetry obscures a meaning that is already muddled in the painting. While repetition makes representation possible, answers are postponed forever. The surface value of the visual image parallels the shallowness of double negatives and rhetorical questions. One form of expression echoes the other, and both of them compound the viewer's perplexity vis-à-vis a language of absence.

There is Flora and flowers in Comanini's poem, but how does one become the other? Flora itself cannot answer; hence the final question: "Do you know how?" Such an impasse betrays a world of words in which questions are exchanged for new doubts. The noun is stated and then denied, while the verse breaks meaning into halves; image and word mystify each other. Although it is sound ("Am I Flora?") and image ("Or am I flowers?") in the same line, the verse fails to remedy the vacuity of language. Interrogation activated a state of pounding elusiveness, and art acted out a rhetoric of intentional hesitation that teased presence and absence, meaning and lack thereof.

For Arcimboldo and Comanini, Flora exists in the autonomous image of her visual presence, and she fails "to tell her story" because the icastic has neither psychological depth nor temporal extension; she can describe herself only in an objectual way that is spatial. Flora's poetic vocabulary is one of self-contained words visually stretched on the page. We therefore move within a mirrorlike imagery. The time had come when literature could support nondiscursive and yet presentational modes of expression. Throughout the sixteenth century in fact, printing fostered the exchange of things for words on the combinatory field of a written language whose "tone of printing" raised problems of epistemology. Attempts at bringing words as near as possible to the stasis of painting favored explorations of the rhetorical syntax of ellipsis, parataxis, and paradoxical indirections.[14]

At the margins of mannerist art, language unsettled the dynamics of discourse. The poem and painting about Flora exploit their own presentational "how," not "what" their narrative content might be. Throughout, the progression of *poesis* has broken down into the rhetorical tropes of synecdoche, metonymy, and tautology, which blur meaning in much the same way as Arcimboldo distorts our response—"*Che miri o sciocco questa mia pittura?*"—to words and images. Verses have traded literary markers for a wealth of "painted words": indeed, a kind of pictorial language. Likewise, Arcimboldo's equation of sound-image-word was but an example of mannerist arrangements that let the arts mix on grounds where meaning could not sink below the written surface.[15]

Taking the metaphor of perspective—we know what we see—quite literally, Sperone Speroni wrote that, like "a painter's helper, the grammarian polishes and arranges words so that the master of rhetoric paints the truth while speaking." Furthermore, "just as physical presence suffices to paint a portrait without requiring any knowledge of personality, so rhetoric suffices to speak of any object of which we know only something." That something was phrased as *un certo non so che* in Ferrara and as *je ne sais quoi* at Fontainebleau. Spelling out a principle to which Arcimboldo and Comanini adhered wholeheartedly, Speroni concluded that the pictorial-rhetorical artifice presents "the exterior surface of physical appearances seen by everybody's eyes."[16] Truth rested with things that taught, whereas beauty stemmed from images that were meant to delight. In the latter's province, forms could either "cross over" from one "code" to another or be lodged between them. Once metaphorical eccentricity became a desirable standard, arrangement exploited permutations of all kinds. In the hands of the grotesque *jongleur,* art built static compounds alien to metamorphosis. Such a playful approach surfaced again in another poem on Flora by Filippo Gherardino:

Né cangiò Flora in Fiori,
Né i Fiori in Flora
Il pittor saggio, ma dipinse Flora
Com'è, Flora di Fiori.

(Neither Flora was changed into Flowers,
Nor were Flowers changed into Flora
By the good painter, who painted Flora
As she is, Flora of Flowers.)

Ostentatiously, lines refer back to each other. Repetition, echoing, and tautology stage a war of words whose epistemological incongruity tests the range of rhetorical virtuosity. Meaning is evaded and what emerges is the icastic image of a floral constellation. The poem pivots on metaphorical transfers of quality (Flora) into quantity (*Fiori*) whereby language denies narrative temporality. Reading bounces back and forth; the beginning is the end, and the last word is the first. Discourse comes to a halt and words stand as inert objects edging on a kind of still-life status. Because the linkage between word and world is suspended, priority is given to what Clayton Koelb calls "lethetic narratives," which "elaborate structures found not in the nonlinguistic world but in the resources of language itself."[17] Linguistic tropes were so engrossed that they became narrative units. Art toyed with strategies of reversibility.

Arcimboldo and Comanini understood that the linguistic mode of rhetorical extravagance neither described nor discovered reality. Instead, it mocked narrativity by exploiting a readable surface on which approval could be gained without any serious commitment to truth. By the same token, the reader-viewer accepts the conventions that rule atopia. As a result, language is more valuable than experience, speech obeys its own laws, and reading is quite prone to turn sense into nonsense. The interdisciplinary virtuosity of such mannerist texts thrived amid tropological spaces in which a proliferation of words lost meaning to stylistic clichés. Inversions of form and content were but signs of the instability of knowledge itself. What triumphed was fiction as fiction, and we can safely guess that Samuel Beckett's Watt would have recited that kind of literature with flair.

VI

Comanini's literary rendition of Vertumnus, who also is Rudolph II (Fig. 19), so echoed the Arcimboldesque approach that an intermedia comparison is mandatory:

> Qual tu sii, che me guardi
> Strana e difforme imago,
> E 'l riso hai su le labbra,
> Che lampeggia per gli occhi
> E tutto 'l volto imprime
> Di novella allegrezza,
> Al veder novo monstro,
> Che Vertunno chiamaro
> Ne' lor carmi gli antichi
> Dotti figli d'Apollo.
>
> (Whoever you might be, who look at me
> As a strange and deformed image,
> Wearing on your lips a smile
> That shines forth through your eyes
> And illuminates your whole face
> With a new happiness

The moment you have seen a new monster,
Which is called Vertumnus
In the poetry of the ancient
And knowledgeable sons of Apollo.)

As the speaking voice, the god is aware of his unbecoming appearance. The grotesque mixture of portraiture with still life foregrounds a complacent paradox:

Se 'n mirar non t'ammiri
Del brutto, ond'io son bello,
Ben non sai qual bruttezza
Avanzi ogni bellezza.

(If in looking you do not admire
That ugliness by which I am beautiful,
You do not know how far ugliness
Stands above beauty.)

Happy compounds—"*lieto miscuglio*"—of deformity and ugliness lost mimesis to stupefying indirections, and the mannerist duplicity of *bello-brutto* exaggerated Leonardo da Vinci's earlier claim: "Beautiful and ugly features are mutually enhancing."[18]

As a figure of multiple—if not mesmerizing—indirections, Vertumnus unveils the "royal sun" hiding a "monster" within. One disguises the other, and the deity reveals to the spectator.

Quel ch'io son, quanto adombro.

(What I am, and what I adumbrate.)

But who is he? Vertumnus, Rudolph, or somebody else? As the French poet Jodelle was writing at that time, the deity's metamorphoses spawned a "*demi-brut, demi-dieu.*" The speaking *I* is conscious of his variety:

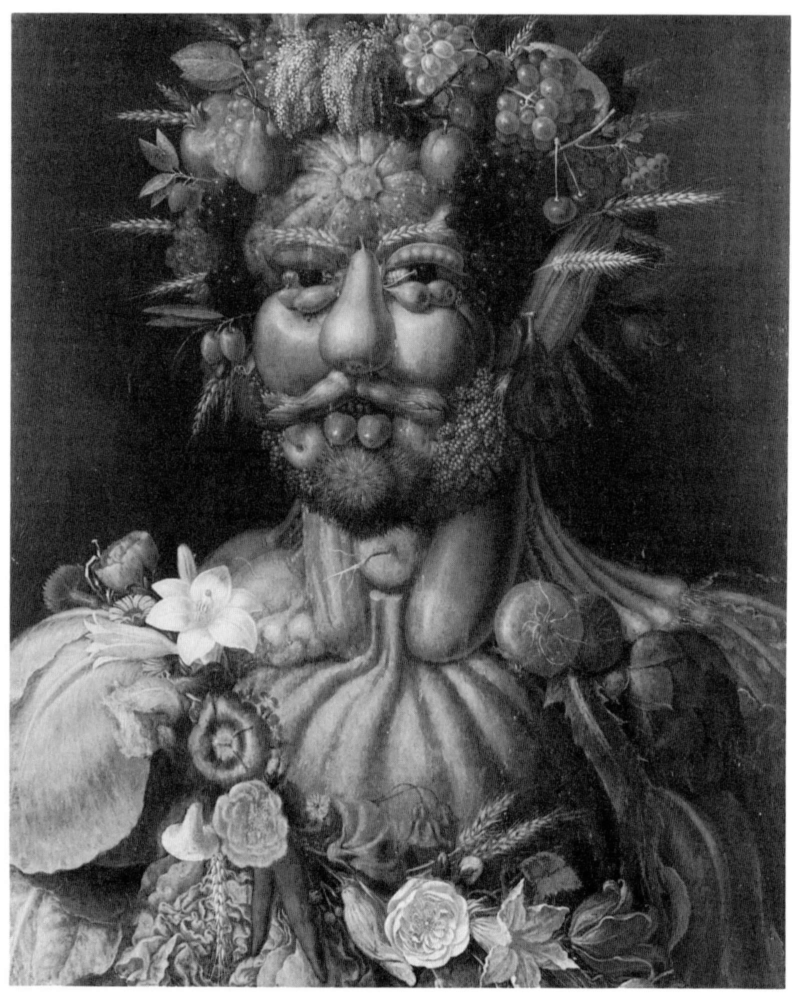

Fig. 19. Giuseppe Arcimboldo, *Vertumnus as Rudolph II*, 1591. Skoklosters Slott, Stockholm

Vario son da me stesso,
E pur, si vario, un solo
Sono, e di varie cose
Col mio vario sembiante
Le sembianze ritraggo.

. . . .

Son, che fuor sembro un mostro,
E dentro alme sembianze
E regia imago ascondo.

. . . .

Or vanne, o Spettatore,
Che 'n pochi carmi ho detto
Quel ch'io son, quanto adombro.

(I appear in different guises from what I am.
Yet, amid such variety, I am
A single figure, and of various things
I can portray a range of resemblances.

. . . .

On the outside, I appear to be a monster,
But a beautiful resemblance
and a royal image I hide inside.

. . . .

Now go, spectator,
Since I have said in few lines
What I am, and What I adumbrate.)

Language weighs on a split between self and other—"*sembiante*" and "*sembianze.*" Although similar, words contradict each other. "*Vario*" asserts plurality in the first line, only to stress the unity of "*un solo*" in the following one. Yet, variety can be true to its own meaning only by refusing to settle into any form; poetry brings together what reality keeps apart. Identity is doubled and words hide meaning instead of revealing it. Pictorial and literary techniques have made it possible to conceive of the self as a plural variety of itself: portrait, myth, and still life. Extravagance on matters of identity could encompass names and types. By means of a technique familiar to Arcimboldo, eccentricity pivots on the factual "self-here"—"*sono*"—adumbrating—"*adombro*"—an improbable "other-there." In both instances, several orders of life are displaced into a spatial vacuum.

Time therefore is abolished and the forms of nature are drained of any residual vitality:

Dimmi or tu, se t'aggrada
Di veder quant'io celo
Ch'or or ne tolgo il velo.

(Tell me if you please
Whether you can see what I hide
For I am just about to remove the veil.)

The unveiling of hidden identity bears on the duplicity of *son-adombro,* which peaks in the line:

Te rassembr'io, te figur'io, te segno

(I resemble you, I am an image of you, I represent you)
(*Trattati,* 3:258–65)

The confrontation-repetition of I-You (*io-tu*) heightens the visual character of verbs working as mirrors that can bounce resemblance back and forth between pronouns. Humanlike presence stirs semantic confusion.

Still in terms of diachronic analogues, the grotesque portrait of Vertumnus–Rudolph II mingles history with nature through a mosaic made up of less than noble tesserae. On archetypal grounds, Arcimboldo fell back on the tradition of hyperbolic allusions to kingship, which have hidden the sacred within the profane: the deity "disfigures" the prince, and both of them are concealed amid a cornucopian harvest of vegetables. Visually, reality conceals fiction. Yet the Arcimboldesque disguise is more than twofold. The array of natural forms stands for Vertumnus; nature "masks" myth. In turn, the deity somehow resembles Rudolph II; myth "masks" history. The anthropomorphic figure therefore hides nature behind both myth and history.

Ovid put forward a logical relationship when he dressed up Vertumnus "as a reaper":

> He would come with hay around his ears and temples
> (*Metamorphoses* xiv)

Likewise, Comanini so described the summerlike makeup of Arcimboldo's god:

> Mira ciò che le tempie
> Mi cinge, orna e colora:
> Tante spiche pungenti,
> Che 'l polveroso Giugno
> Matura, indora e coce.
> (260)

> (You ought to admire
> What I wrapped around my temples:
> They are many stinging acorns
> Which dusty June
> Matures, warms, and ripens into a golden color.)

At the same time, the picture is a portrait and an antiportrait. Even the order of portraiture could be turned around; reality became fictional and fiction could be mimetic. We approach here what Mircea Eliade has called a "dialectic of camouflage,"[19] whose paradoxical structure warrants reversals of all sorts.

Grotesque deities well served to conceal identity at a time when a Neapolitan sonnet so praised Giovanna Castriota:

> Altra Pale, altra Flora, altra Pomona,
> altra Cerere abbiam

> (We have another Pale, another Flora, another Pomona, another Ceres)

The self is played against the cumulative "otherness" of an onomastic field in which names double themselves (Pale = Ceres) and novelty exists "in the manner of," or "in excess of," older mythology.[20]

VII

At the outer edges of the figurative web of Western culture, *imitazione fantastica* and *credible maraviglioso* strained the link between mimesis and originality. In turn, adumbration of nature and *proporzione–locuzione–sprezzatura artificiosa* pushed art to the limit of both rhetoric and representation. Mannerism flaunted its eccentric "marginality."

Recent criticism of drama and the novel has focused on art at the boundary. On the "mannerist" subject of miniature, Gaston Bachelard told us a while ago that we "are forced to cross the threshold of absurdity."[21] On matters of literary liminality, Gustavo Pérez Firmat writes that, "of late, margins have been everywhere. . . . Contemporary reflection in literary studies and related disciplines (anthropology and philosophy especially) has been powerfully drawn to diverse manifestations of the marginal, to phenomena that, in Victor Turner's words, fall 'betwixt and between the positions assigned and arrayed by law, custom, convention and ceremonial.' "[22] Neither temporary nor transitional, liminality sets up a position of eccentricity vis-à-vis a given center, against which it describes the inverted world of carnival, disease, and social subversion.

Reversals and disease are part of the broader experience of Mannerism, from the painter's sickness in Comanini's treatise to the psychological obsessions of Pontormo, Rosso Fiorentino, and Bronzino. Francesco I's *studiolo* in Palazzo della Signoria is emblematic of a paradoxical liminality at the core of public power. It was his obsession to shy away from people. For that reason, Vasari had to build a corridor over Ponte Vecchio so that the Duke could move between residences on both sides of the Arno river without mingling with people. The *studiolo* itself had no windows, and only candles could shed light on a world of inner illuminations framed by pictures on every wall. Because it parodied both center and periphery, such an enclave of individual and artistic autonomy was intrinsically disruptive. In a most ironic way, Mannerist marginality outdid itself by lodging a symbol of claustrophobic privacy in the very seat of government.

At heart, liminality is disruptive, for it "consistently threatens to collapse the center-periphery distinction." It is a "structure that subverts structure." Yet it can occur only where structures of order stand up. Francesco I's obsession with privacy was due in large part to the public nature of his office. As Mikhail Bakhtin taught us, the carnivalesque "misrule" parodies the "rule" in much the same way as Vasari linked *regola* to *licenzia.*[23]

In a mannerist key, to cross the threshold of common sense, to trespass gravity at the ground floor, to court the ex-centric, the surreal, the miniature, and the gigantic, is to let excess have its way. To make proportion artificial is to let the artist possess the world at the margins of both logic and experience, where art takes charge of an unproportional reality of its own making.

As any margin, the artist's own margin has two sides: the artless and the artful. One is deficient, the other excessive. Within the liminal topography of Mannerism, the deficient edged on the early crisis of faith that seized Pontormo and Rosso Fiorentino. The excessive mapped out its bizarre realm, first and foremost at Bomarzo. Its antiworld, Marcello Fagiolo suggests, is rooted in the *aldilà,* namely, the other side of classical history because of the preexistence of Etruscan contaminations; the other side of Western geography because of exotic longings; and the other side of perspectival space because of sensational effects.[24]

In the culture of Mannerism, however, "adumbration of nature" did cast its shadows at the last threshold where the "anti" and the "counter" would not leave the vestiges of the figurative world behind. The "ex-centric" was still linked to the center, much as artificiality was out to circumvent mimesis. As a result, the spectacle of liminality became ever more spectacular, and art took the greatest delight in its own artfulness.

4

Mannerism and the Fabric of Adorable Improbabilities

Weaving elaborate verbal snares may stand as typical of the attitude that governs poems in the mannerist mode, which insists that whatever else art may be, it is first of all art, even at the risk of being manierato. *And although it may create and inhabit its own world of imaginative works and its first allegiance must be to itself, art, even thus defined as autonomous and self-referential, is also a part of experience, if only as a negative exemplum.*

—James V. Mirollo

Part I

I

Surprise and novelty aside, mannerist *capricci* were not meant to teach lessons somehow applicable to life. While setting emulation free of mimesis, art shaped an autonomous realm in which progress cherished distinctive styles that "outdid" tradition. For Arcimboldo and Comanini, technique was a matter of novelty, and style thrived on "routine" virtuosity. Manner, Walter Friedlaender warns, "repeats something predetermined," which is what happened during the second half of the sixteenth century from Florence and Prague to Fontainebleau.[1] Repetitiveness implied quantification and excess. It was easier to act artificially than naturally in the intransitive province of delectation, and we ought to bear in mind that the very term *manierismo* refers to artificial stylizations of great models.[2]

Early in the sixteenth century, it was assumed that style implied poise, elegance, and performance, which cast a negative light on unnaturalness, affectation, and self-consciousness. As the century unfolded, fantastic imitation drew opposites closer; Castiglione's *sprezzatura* gave way to the *sprezzatura artificiosa* of Comanini, and Vasari's concept of artistic license stood at the other side, but not beyond, the reach of rules: "*Nella regola una licenzia.*" Ultimately, success led Arcimboldo to make license itself normative.[3]

II

To set Mannerism apart from the Baroque, some basic distinctions ought to be drawn. While Vasari and Comanini linked originality to experimentation, Bruno took on the whole structure of genre theory in 1584–85: "Poetry is not born of the rule, except by the merest chance, but that the rules derive from the poetry. For that reason there are as many genres and species of true rules as there are of true poets."[4] He thus faced a dilemma: How could one sustain anticanonical stands without transforming them into new canons? How could one challenge the rigidity of a system without setting up an antisystem equally inflexible? From Bruno and Cervantes to Velázquez, much art set creation and criticism on parodic grounds somehow equidistant from generic and antigeneric poles. Often the critique of creation was part of the creative act itself. Whereas baroque forms strove to move away from generic grips, the mannerist artifice bathed itself in its successful repetitiveness.

Lodged as it was between pictorial ambiguity and linguistic indirections, the mannerist Flora visualized a kind of parasitic growth that fed on Humanism but rejected the new life system of the Baroque. Bruno was committed to "make everything of everything" because he believed in a transformational view of life. Conversely, Arcimboldo's bizarre arrangements stood at bay of empirical processes; artifice had to turn away from nature. Instead of roaming freely through the infinity of the New Science, the mannerist sphynx stayed put on grounds where nature became artistic, artful, and artificial.[5]

Focusing on the sixteenth century, Craig Hugh Smyth writes that Maniera resulted from three major causes: "The first cause was uncomprehending, and mostly exclusive, imitation of some previous style—that of Michelangelo principally, but in some case of Raphael or Correggio, or of antique sculpture. Second was routine dexterity gained through practice, but only superficial and mechanical dexterity, because of haste and lack of knowledge. And third was an admixture of extravagance and caprice." Arcimboldo's art, I think, would be compatible with the second and third cause. The critic goes on to say that "the anti-classical style of the twenties was born chiefly of the desire to experiment and contribute something new, rather than from spiritual crisis. It was experiment amid many experiments at that moment in the history of painting more than out-and-out revolt."[6] Yet, the anticlassical experimentalism of Pontormo and Rosso Fiorentino was not the only one in a period of seventy turbulent years.[7]

After the middle of the sixteenth century, the fantastic in art gained strength. Dürer had appreciated diversity and "numberless differing opinions about beauty," and Leonardo da Vinci also demanded variety. Especially in northern Italy, Erwin Panofsky reminds us, many an artist set out to outdo the classical style in the thick of a culture with an appetite for amusements of all kinds.[8] Amid that extravagant constellation of forms, we may call attention to sculptural hybrids such as the bronze satyrs by Giambologna in a grotto at Pratolino (Fig. 20) or in Ammanati's Fountain of Neptune (1563–75, Florence), the monstrous frames of Federico Zuccari for the Palazzetto Zuccari in Rome (Fig. 21),

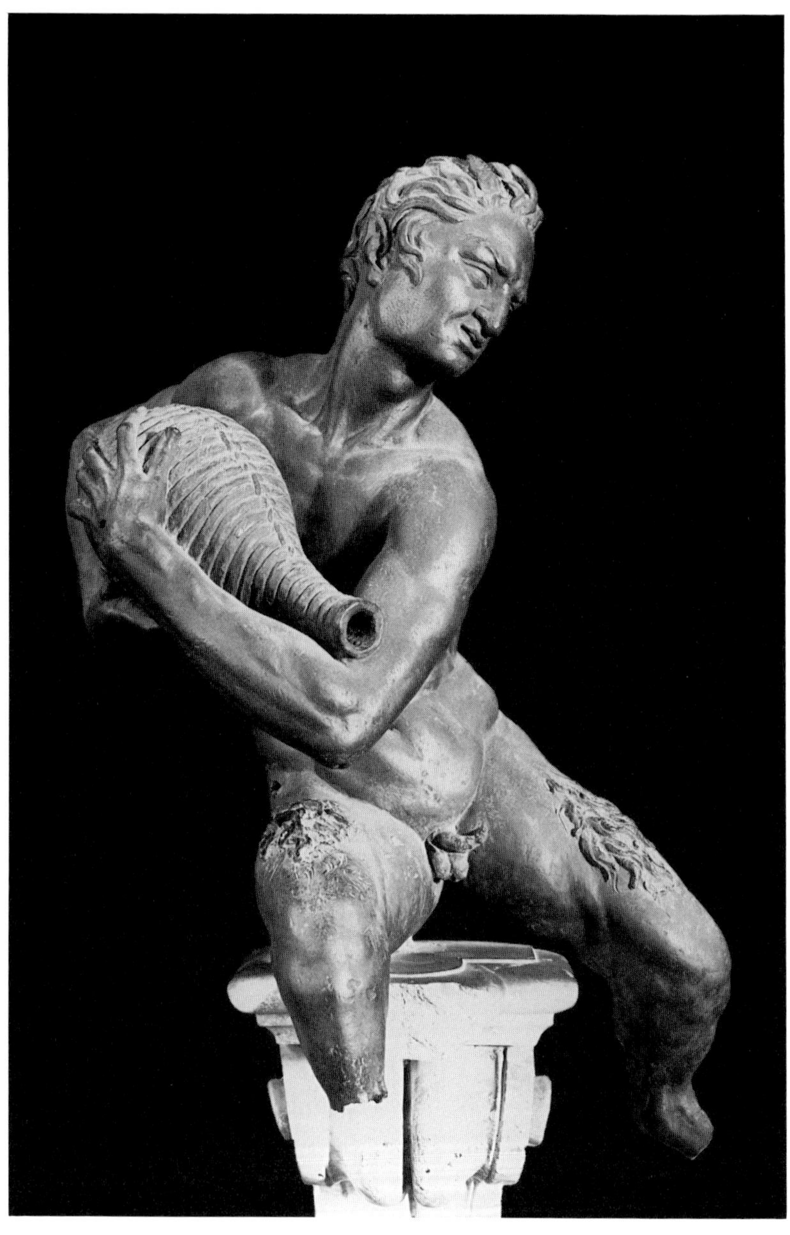

Fig. 20. Giambologna, *Bronze Satyr* from a grotto at Pratolino. Museo Nazionale, Florence

and the anamorphic distortion of Parmigianino's *Self-Portrait in a Convex Mirror* (1524, see Fig. 12).

Criticism has set the stylized art of Mannerism during the last quarter of the sixteenth century against the realistic concreteness of the Baroque.[9] Such a parallelism suggests that the evolution of culture can thrive on progress and stagnation at the same time. It is a critical fallacy to presume that periods—or movements—ought to follow one another as single links in a chain.

III

To make specific comparisons between Mannerism and the Baroque, I shall focus on metamorphosis, a radical form of change and eccentricity that is central to the poetics of both. In a baroque context, Bruno could see "in the faces of many in the human species expressions, voices, gestures, affects, and inclinations, some equine, others asinine, aquiline, and bovine." They all exuded "a vital principle which, by virtue of the proximate past or proximate future mutations of bodies, they have been or are about to be pigs, horses, asses, eagles, or whatever else they indicate."[10] Organic mutations in Bernini's *Apollo and Daphne* (1622–25; Fig. 22) turn legs into bark, toes into roots, and hair into leaves. Likewise, Marino's sonnet "*Donna che si pettina*" transforms hair into sea waves. Innate to literary and sculptural form, the metamorphic process unfolds in time and space.[11]

By contrast, Arcimboldo's metamorphoses are intellectual constructs. Metaphor in *The Water* (see Fig. 8) links the details of marine life to the verbal category; change is muted into contiguity. Although they seem to parallel the natural mutations of worms into butterflies, such ensembles in fact parody metamorphosis by confusing a functional organism with a mechanical assemblage. Neither the transformational powers of nature nor those of language are operative in the mannerist artwork, whose unity is decorative rather than energetic. In discussing the metamorphic powers of dream-world deities, Comanini writes that Arcimboldo emulated them (*Trattati,*

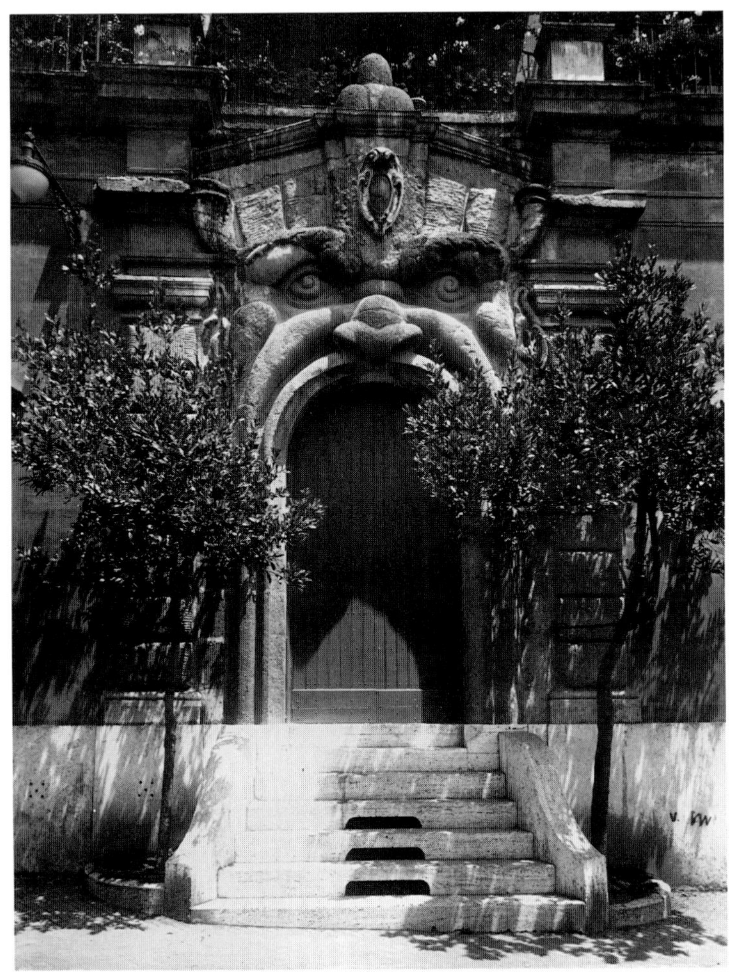

Fig. 21. Federico Zuccari, Palazzetto Zuccari (detail). Via Gregoriana, Rome

3:270) through composition—"*componendo,*" conjunction—"*congiungersi,*" and mixture—"*accozzando,*" all of which work at the surface. Eccentricity was limited to superficial displacements.[12] With an eye to what Isidore of Seville called etymological *heteromorphia,* his figures "involve a change of position without transformation" (*Etymologiae* XI.3.9).

At this point we ought to bear in mind that Aristotle set static and active metaphors apart: "To say that a good man is 'four-squared' is certainly a metaphor; both the good man and the square are perfect; but the metaphor does not suggest activity. On the other hand, in the expression 'with his vigour in full bloom' there is a notion of activity" (*Rhetoric* 1411b, 26–30). The distinction between animate and inanimate tropes—Bernini versus Arcimboldo—could therefore help us to draw a line between the "mutable" Baroque, which respects the organic integrity of the object, and "composite" Mannerism, which makes form depend exclusively on the subject who arranges it. Rhetorical tropes are therefore functional in one case and structural in the other.

I think that it would be more appropriate at this point to look at Arcimboldo's portraits as collages. Whether surrealist or dadaist, such a technique rounded a variety of objects on the surface in a way that each one of them maintains its autonomy vis-à-vis the whole. Because it favors spatial simultaneity over the ingrained narrativity of reliefs and mosaics, the collage foregrounds a decorative technique meant to "cohere well" on the flat surface. The order of the world could be reduced to that of the canvas, much as the order of the printed page was developing its own surfacelike semantics at a time when a typographical culture made it possible for the visual to come into its own.[13]

Turning the compass of rhetoric to points of iconography, Mario Praz writes that Arcimboldo mixed noble subject with prosaic vocabulary in *Vertumnus as Rudolph II,* who "shares Proteus' mutability, only that Proteus already represents absolute mutability with exploitation of forms, which is generally considered typical of baroque modes of expression." Ovid and Horace tell us that he could "change himself into any shape" because he was "the god of the multiple changes" (*Metamor-*

phoses XIV, *Satires* II). Vertumnus, instead, is "more restrained; his experiments with mutation have a precise goal in mind." Since his metamorphoses are limited to the four seasons, the deity seems to stand for an artistic approach midway between stability and transformation. Well within the operative gap of mannerist techniques,[14] his mutations are predictable.

At this juncture, it is quite relevant to note that Erasmus anchored his defense of "the abundance of subject matter" in the second book of *De copia* to a mythology of "changeableness" that included figures of transformation such as Mercury, Circe, Morpheus, Vertumnus, and Proteus. The latter two add luster to variations of hyperboles and superlatives: "More inconstant than Vertumnus," who "gets his name from the fact that he is continually changing—*vertere*—his form," and more mutable than Proteus, "who transforms himself into all kinds of incredible things" (Book 1, 46). Inconstancy is measured by seasons that do not last. Pivoting on recurrence and denial, instability could be patterned. Erasmus would thus support Praz's reading, granted a few godly hybrids here and some grotesque transfers there.

At the beginning of the sixteenth century, even as influential a theorist as Pietro Bembo placed limits on the "changeableness" of the Protean myth: "The ancient poets seem to have fashioned Proteus first as water, then as fire, and then as a beast; yet he never showed more than one form at a time, not only because they did not think this could be done but because they did not see how those things could be joined properly."[15] As a humanist, he relied on intellectual classifications rather than organic processes. The contrast between Proteus and Vertumnus therefore weighs on a qualitative difference, namely, metamorphosis as either an organic process or a construct assembled in the *officina* of mental extravagance. One is transitive and physiologically functional; things become other things. The other is intransitive and inherently self-referential; things are like or unlike other things.[16]

Half a century later, Tasso transferred the Protean myth to aesthetic grounds in one of his *intermedi*, which were allegorical

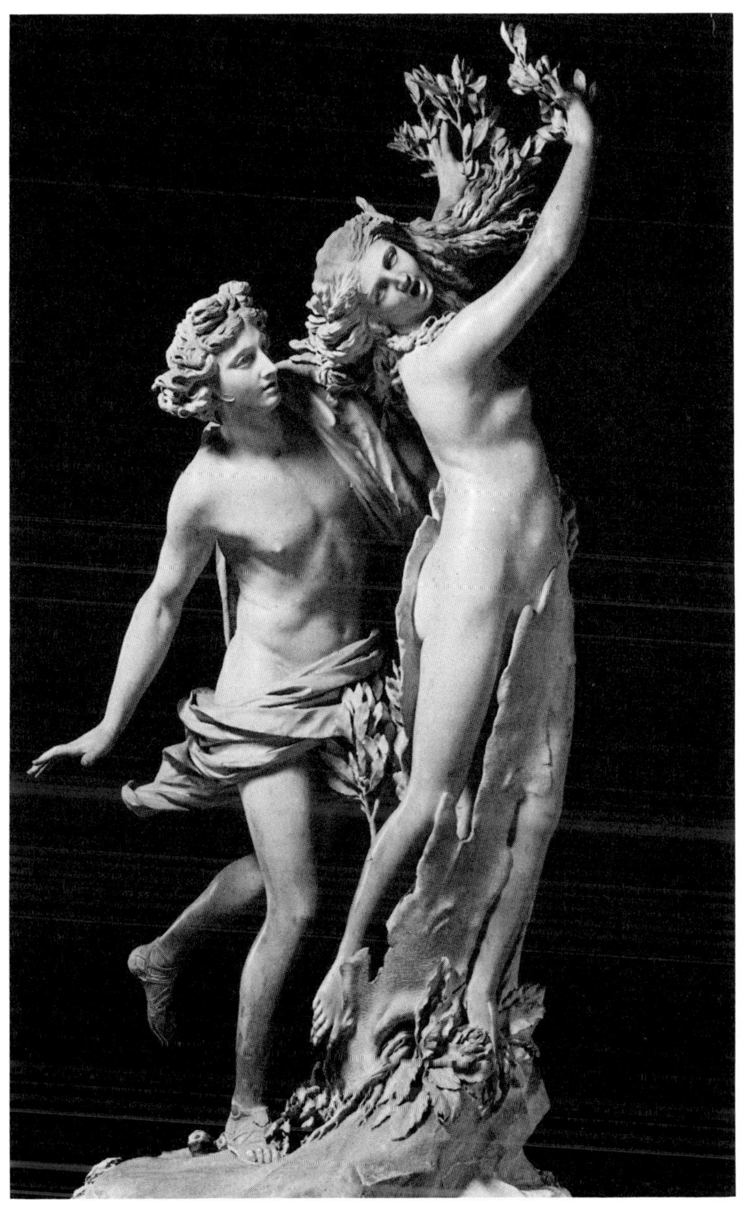

Fig. 22. Gianlorenzo Bernini, *Apollo and Daphne,* 1622–24. Galleria Borghese, Rome

representations with musical accompaniment inserted between the acts of stage performances:

> Proteo son io, che trasmutar sembianti
> e forme soglio variar si spesso.
>
> (I am Proteus, who transforms resemblances
> and keeps changing forms very often)

Because he is the god of scene changes, Proteus presides over the world of theatrical artifice.[17]

On the subject of metamorphosis, Tasso wrote at the end of his dialogue on beauty:

> Without any doubt, I esteem that what is unstable and inconstant is to be equated with a liar; since the man who makes innumerable mutations of appearance, custom, age, is not a real man, just as the boy is not a man . . . but the real man rather is an image and a fantastic construct of human essence. . . . Only that which never changes, varies, or undergoes increase and diminution but always remains the same and resembles itself is true. In fact, all things that depend on generation and corruption are false.[18]

Even at that late stage of sixteenth-century culture, metamorphosis stirred disruption at the periphery of humanist stability. When Santi di Tito painted *Le sorelle di Fetonte mutate in pioppi* in Francesco I's *studiolo,* hands and hair stretch out into leafy twigs attached to the body; no transformation takes place, and the metamorphosis falls back on literary sources.[19]

Bruno, instead, invested his Protean verb *fare* (to make) with a plastic energy that was at once metaphoric and metamorphic: "It is possible to convert any fable, romance, dream and prophetic enigma, and to employ it by virtue of metaphor and allegorical disguise in such a way as to signify all that pleases him who is skillful at tugging at the sense, and is thus adept at making everything of everything."[20] Whereas Bruno broke the old circle of Ptolemaic unity, the fantastic virtue of the mannerists aborted teleological concerns with the future. They took refuge in a maze of their own making, where Arcimboldo could play with everything. Both minds were cornucopian; however, one chose "generation," while the other settled with "construction." In nature, growth is self-regulatory and abnormality cannot be permanent. The man-made, instead, can imitate growth, but it also can turn to alternatives either deficient or excessive. It was a mannerist undertaking to make what nature could not. Yet, growth and assemblage could claim equal permanence in art.

IV

On mannerist grounds, Vasari traced the origin of painting and sculpture back to the Etruscans. Although buried "between the walls of the Labyrinth," the marvelous tomb of Porsena at Chiusi revealed "some terracotta tiles in half-relief of such fine workmanship and style that they could not be the products of an immature art." In the preface to the *Lives,* a link was established between "labyrinthine artforms" and the maturity of artists who had "skill and ability." Labyrinthine maps could only be chartered at the margins of nature and far from primitivism.

Interesting connections have been made between the labyrinth and a mannerist assortment of natural and man-made forms. Natural labyrinths such as the Grotte di Postumia display rock formations in the guise of elephant heads, turtles, and galleries of crystals. The fauna living there includes unusual hybrids that can breathe above as well as under water.[21]

Aside from misnaming roses, Umberto Eco has drawn a line between mazes and labyrinths. The classical labyrinth is linear. Theseus "could not but reach the center, and from the center the way out." While Ariadne's thread is in fact useless, the Minotaur is there "to make the whole thing a little more exciting."

The labyrinth therefore would be baroque insofar as linearity and continuity depart from, and go back to, the outside world. On referential grounds, the labyrinth evokes mystery and points back to Crete and the Minotaur. Even Shakespeare linked it to tradition:

> Thou mayest not wander in that labyrinth;
> There minotaur and ugly treason lurk.
> (*Henry IV*, 5.3)

The maze, instead, "is a Mannerist invention; iconologically speaking, it does not appear before the late Renaissance. A maze," Eco goes on to say, "displays choices between paths, some of which led to dead ends."[22] For Borges, the word "maze" calls forth "amazement," which links its ludic connotations to games, puzzles, and garden amusements. Mannerist mazes at Pratolino, Bagnaia, and the Boboli Gardens in Florence offered amusements of all sorts by exploiting nature and technology alike. Outdoors, mannerist fancies created a "chalky wildlife, dwarfs, deformities, and ragamuffins all enjoying themselves in rough games, sour music, and crude laughter."[23] In Rome, the mazelike architecture of Castel Sant'Angelo treasured a *summa* of mannerist art. While Perin del Vaga painted "grottesche" in the papal quarters, pyrotechnics provided surreal disguises on festive occasions.

Labyrinths are unicursal, whereas mazes tend to be multicursal, for they refer to fortresses, hiding places, or sanctuaries filled with terror. Such a cumulative structure of formal patterns is indeed representative of the mannerist frame of mind. To be "mazed" is to enter an "interplay of identities" and to be amusingly "mazed in one another," which is visually the case with the portrait of Vertumnus–Rudolph II (see Fig. 19). Michael Ayrton would agree that mazes test choice, confusion, and ambiguity to the limits of endurance. The maze in fact is "a model of the brain, a diagram of the intestines, a map of the world."[24] In the maze we are protected and imprisoned by our own ingenuity, which has created a design of excessive indirections.

V

In the liminal province of mannerist self-indulgence, the artist resisted the ideological flow of historical progress that Bruno, Caravaggio, and Bernini accepted wholeheartedly. At the margins of that flux, the mannerists fell back on the ludic potential of the artistic tradition itself. A poetics rooted in such ideological assumptions would indeed take the maze as a metaphorical marker of willful indirections. To better understand the mannerist character and function of the maze, I think that it would be helpful to focus on its kindred source: Daedalus's mythic labyrinth in Crete.

For Theseus, the labyrinth represents a challenge, which he meets. He enters it, performs a heroic deed, and then leaves the island. The construction bodies forth a man-made test of human prowess; it is a microcosmic equivalent of the epic wilderness. Theseus and Daedalus are men of destiny. In a way, they challenge each other in Crete, only to leave it in order to pursue their appointed destinies. The geographical marginality of the island is as symbolic as their departure from it. The labyrinth is a stage on which the *homo artifex* proves himself, and by so doing he changes his life. Having found and defeated his match at the center of architectural deviations, the labyrinth, Theseus enters the realm of legend. The labyrinth is the locus of fateful tests.

It is equally important to this study that the Minotaur appeared on the scene when Cretan civilization had started to wane. Pasiphaë was taken by excessive desire, Daedalus fled, the enraged Minos went after him only to be killed, and Ariadne helped a stranger to rid the island of the monster. Excesses and displacements of that kind would indeed qualify as "mannerist" markers of mythological decline.

In a mannerist key, some kind of reversal should be expected. Our focus therefore ought to shift from the transitive journey of Theseus to the static permanence of the Minotaur. From the monster's standpoint, the building creates a structure that isolates the center. Like a spider, he stands at the core of a symbolic form of marginality that isolates him from the external world.

He is at home there, does not get lost in it, and wants to keep it that way. The architectural cobweb provides him with safety and shelter; it is "another" world for us, not for the Minotaur.

At an earlier humanist stage, Alberti equated the ideal family leader with a spider: "You know the spider and how he constructs his web. All the threads spread out in rays, each of which, however long, has its source, its roots or birthplace, as we might say, at the center. From there each filament starts and moves outward. The most industrious creature himself then sits at that spot and has his residence there. . . . Let the father of a family do likewise."[25] While dismissing the spider as a pedagogical model of social behavior, Arcimboldo would have admired the industriousness of a creature weaving labyrinthine filaments. Later, Francis Bacon would look on those threads as decorative intricacies and rhetorical tangles that we would consider mannerist indeed. On the way to Bacon, the mannerist spider did not build structures of order but ornamental patterns that thrived on aestheticism.

In real life, spiders have to pin their filaments to the phenomenal instability of the outside world. They lodge themselves in quiet places where atmospheric activity is minimal, so that they can spin their web in an empty vacuum as abstract as a perspectival grid. At the very edge of lifelessness, cobwebs thrive in corners of dusty inertia quite marginal to the biological mainstream of life. In such a mannerist displacement, the cobweb is aesthetically beautiful; in point of fact, it is a trap. And so could the mannerist spell become, if one were to overlook its artificiality.

At the center of the architectural cobweb, the Minotaur is a hybrid whose contacts with the outside are minimal. Unlike Theseus and Daedalus, he has no future to build; initiative and ingenuity are beyond his reach. He shall never cross the threshold of history, and he can only perform repetitive acts—indeed, the physical and behavioral markers of a mannerist mode.

Although a hybrid animal, the Minotaur is condemned to live in a man-made environment. As the offspring of human transgression, he can appease his appetite only through human sacrifice. Man's use and abuse of his own ingenuity could therefore feed on each other. And that metaphorical leap cannot fail to echo the mannerist penchant for exploiting the output of the artistic tradition. For the mannerist parasite does not grow on trees, but on walls and other man-made artifacts.

If the Minotaur ever wanted to get out of the labyrinth, he would be lost. In other words, the man-made cobweb was there to protect his isolation rather than to prevent his escape. It was Ariadne's thread, therefore, that drew a line between labyrinth and maze. The thread was a link back to the transitive patterns of history; the lack of it maintained an intransitive isolation that was deliberate.

If at all needed, the mannerist thread would be spun within the building itself; not to find a sense of direction but to tease that very idea. Since Daedalus himself almost got trapped in it, the Cretan building was in fact a maze, which kept the Minotaur safe. Unfortunately for him, it did happen that Theseus on one fatal occasion transformed it into a labyrinth. After all, parasitic existence is subordinate; eventually any Minotaur would find his Theseus, just as any Arcimboldo would meet his Bruno. At any rate, differences between labyrinths and mazes are more a matter of usage than of plan. In terms of a historical overview, the categorical marginality of the maze is enduring, even though the path of historical progress would eventually displace it.

Part II

I

In 1936 André Breton claimed that the crisis of the object in art could be resolved only through the breakdown of the barriers that separated the *déjà vu* and the "commonly proved from the provable. . . . In this regard, modern scientific artistic thought presents the same structure: the real has been too long confused with the given, for one like the other spreads out in all directions of the possible."[26] Accordingly, originality should replace imitation, while the experience of *déjà vu* could expand into the unlimited possibilities of the fantastic.

In that same year, Alfred J. Barr, Jr., included Arcimboldo in the catalogue for the show "Fantastic Art, Dada, and Surrealism," held at the Museum of Modern Art in New York. Arcimboldo's reversible *Tradition of: Landscape Head* was set next to Dali's equally reversible *Paranoiac Face* (1935), even though the critic cautioned that "many of the fantastic and apparently Surrealist works of the Baroque or the Renaissance are to be explained on *rational* grounds rather than on a Surrealist basis of subconscious and irrational expression."[27]

Such reservations notwithstanding, one could place Arcimboldo's "technological" portraits of *The Genius of Cooking* (see Fig. 13) and *The Librarian* (see Fig. 11) along—or at the start of—a line including Pieter Bruegel's *The Fight of the Money Bags and the Strong Boxes* (1558–67), the *Cubist Designs* of Cambiaso, Bracelli's tennis players made out of tennis rackets (*Capricci,* 1624), Giorgio de Chirico's modern manikins, and the mechanical men of Léger and Duchamp. For a long time, man has found it fit to project himself into older *automi* and more recent robotlike "others" immune to the physiology of growth.

Surviving those who write books and build civilizations, Arcimboldo's librarian and the archaeologists of de Chirico are symbolic of a sustained emphasis on objects instead of ideas. One's dehumanized portraits seem to be prophetic of the other's commitment "to see everything, even man, in its quality of thing."[28]

Things overshadowed values in Arcimboldo's universe, where tomes build up *The Librarian* in a way that is strikingly similar to de Chirico's *The Archaeologists* (1929; Fig. 23). The "metaphysical" canvas consists of nothing but the objects of the researcher's findings, which are housed in a sort of room-museum where anatomy contains the bones of man-history. Within the conventional order of things, archaeologists and museums set antiquity out of its historical context. As such, archaeology restricts the past to the evidence of a fragmentary morphology that has outlasted its makers. Since they are no longer functional, ruins can be displaced into statuesque figures seated in a most eccentric living room. They seem to be either inhabitants or spectators but not art treasures. While dislocations of that sort magnify an enigmatic stillness, archaeology is scaled down to a miniature world in which things are out of proportion and out of place. Both artists fell back on metonymy and metaphor to construct portraits with objects related to their booklike and ruinlike natures.

For Arcimboldo, the *studiolo* no longer was a place of intellectual speculation but a room where tomes were catalogued and archaeological pieces might be kept. Even though they stand where the instruments of learning are gathered, archaeologists and librarian neither take in nor act out knowledge. Without names, they exist as shell-like forms of a professional otherness.

Committed as he was to stretch the resources of perspective. Arcimboldo carved an ideological vacuum in which technique reigned supreme. In the case of reversible figures such as *The Man and the Vegetables* (see Fig. 2), space turned into an a-gravitational chessboard that upstaged history and reality alike. Even de Chirico was committed to defy the predictable, and he often used perspective as a kind of distorted quotation. In his paintings, as Roberto Longhi told us long ago, the fifteenth century became the stage setting for a metaphysical puppet opera with stone guests.

If we were to take "surprise" as a measure of *différence,* Arcimboldo's pots and pans would be related more directly to the kitchen than squares and triangles are to Hector, seers, and metaphysicians in the canvases of de Chirico. Because of a lack of ideological depth, Arcimboldo stood beside tradition and had to deny space as process. De Chirico, instead, so disrupted normal relationships that his painted furniture in an open landscape—*Furniture in the Valley* (Fig. 24)—reminded Jean Cocteau of a house dismantled while the owner was eating his lunch. Everything could be suspect in such a *dépaysagiste,* who also paved public squares with indoor planks. Sydney Freedberg's comments on Maniera art also bear on surrealist kinships: "The existence of the whole image, essentially abstracting as it may be, is asserted by the extreme truth of disparate fragments of it.

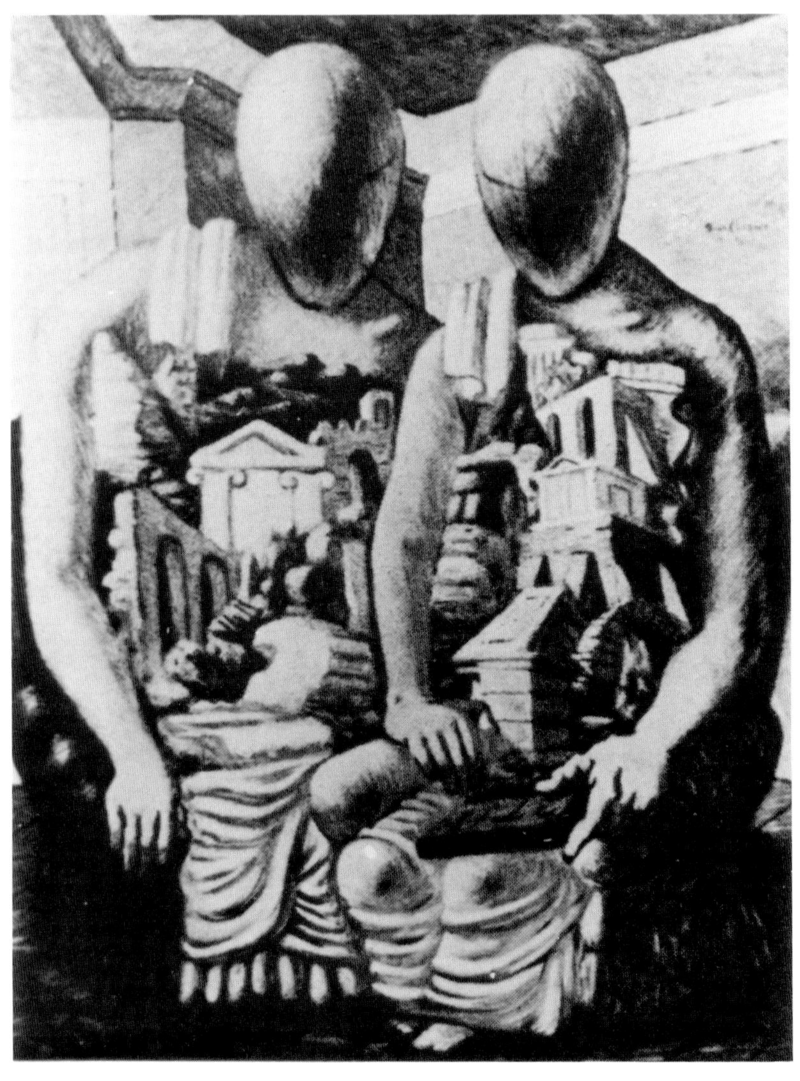

Fig. 23. Giorgio de Chirico, *The Archaeologists,* 1929. Private collection

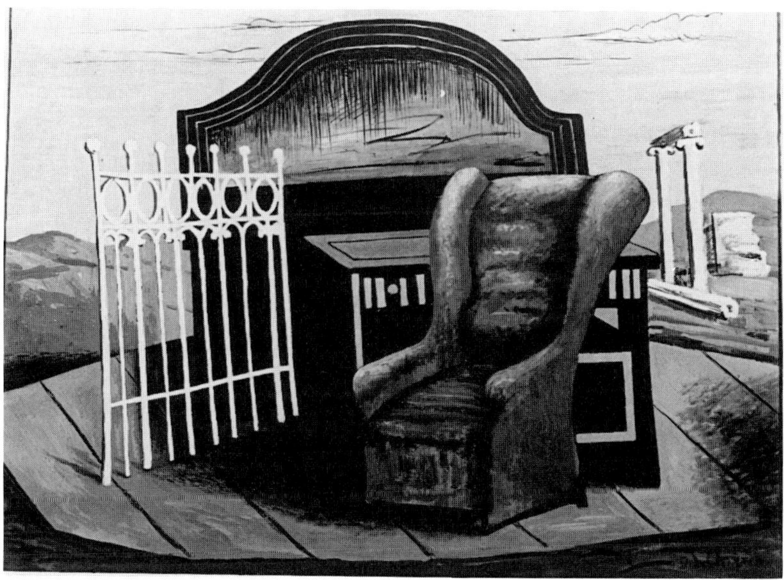

Fig. 24. Giorgio de Chirico, *Furniture in the Valley,* 1927. Private collection

By a device since familiar to the later literature of fantasy, and to modern surrealism, we are baited with the small verity to swallow the whole poetic lie."[29]

II

The verity of details was juxtaposed to the lie of would-be portraits. Humanism's anthropomorphic worldview had evidently reached a point of exaggeration and exhaustion. In its humanlike guise, Arcimboldo's *Genius of Cooking* (see Fig. 13) is none of the objects that it enfolds, even though they all build it up. Although he foreshadowed affinities that the mature Magritte would find between leaf and tree, Arcimboldo could not endorse more radical dissociations between names and things. In front of Magritte's representation of a pipe that is not a pipe (*Ceci n'est*

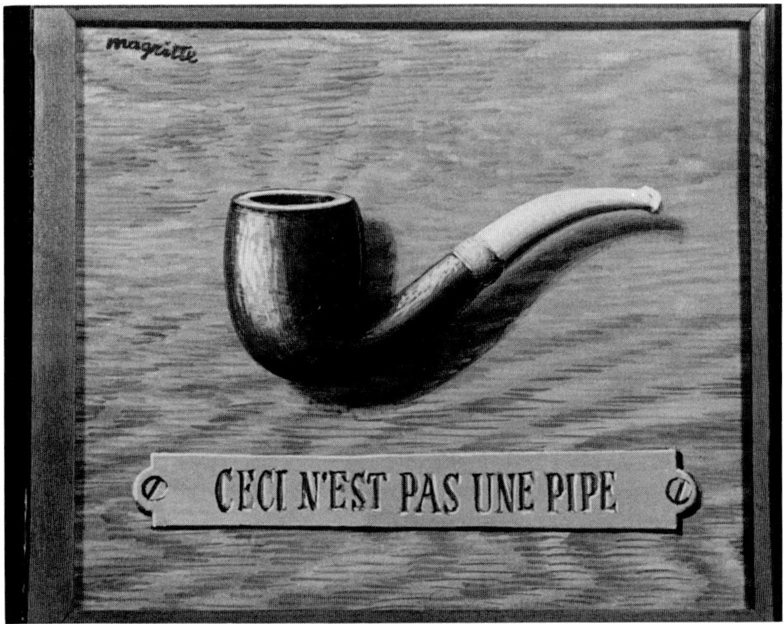

Fig. 25. René Magritte, *Ceci n'est pas une pipe,* 1926. Private collection. Photo courtesy of Draeger, Maître Imprimeur

pas une pipe, 1926; Fig. 25), Arcimboldo would have enjoyed the play on duplicity. If a pipe could not be a pipe, it had to be a figurative object nonetheless.

For Michel Foucault, the phrase "*ceci n'est pas une pipe*" means "this picture, this written phrase, this drawing of a pipe, all this is not a pipe."[30] By the same token, the verbal image-description denies the object as a reality while validating it as art object, that is to say, an artifice. A break between word and sight took place. The text became a test, and representation leaned toward obscurity instead of familiarity. In the mannerist gap between word and image, meaning took up its own negative; doubt was but one aspect of the many dislocations of artistic discourse.

Vertumnus–Rudolph II and de Chirico's double portrait, *Self-*

Portrait (1924; Fig. 26) echoed a language that would utter *Je est un autre* for Rimbaud and *Je m'appelle maintenant tu* with Tristan Tzara. The icastic was uncoded and handed over to arbitrariness. Metaphorical dissociations tested the very concept of "connectedness."

While maintaining analogical ties between leaf and tree, shoe and foot, the titles of Magritte gave visual metaphors a more enigmatic twist. In the case of works such as *L'incendie* (1943) or *La philosophie dans le boudoir* (1947), the puzzle became a riddle. Often the surrealist "similar" leaned toward the fantastic, where the *déjà vu* yielded to the never seen. To gain an edge on the mystery of life, the image was "not an end, but the only means" for clashes of ideas.[31]

However grotesque, Arcimboldo's world is anchored to pictorial resemblance. The bond between title and representation is causal in his canvases, where synecdoches in *The Winter* (see Fig. 1) and metonymies in *The Fire* (see Fig. 9) retain logical ties with their titles. He dislocated objects without letting the unsystematic take the upper hand. Had they been available to Arcimboldo, umbrellas and sewing machines would not have been placed on a table, since his metaphorical artifice, to follow Mario Praz, stood "on this side of common sense."[32]

Added to Magritte's search of mystery, the recurrent keywords in de Chirico's early titles are "infinite," "inconsistency," "disquiet," "mystery," "surprise," "anguish," and "melancholy"; they spell out a cluster of ambiguities. For him, the "known order" was a necessary screen hiding unknown, and better, truths.[33] Arcimboldo instead limited himself to posterlike allegories that immediately revealed the rules of his fictional games. At first, the mannerist turned away from reality and denied any other possible realm before the surrealist began to look for other worlds. Likewise, one mastered simple puzzles before the other ventured to tackle the more complex method of enigma. Such differences are as revealing as the disjunctive grammar that their pictorial languages shared.

In 1919 de Chirico wrote that "spiritual impotence leads to naturalism and fatally reduces painting to a slapshed negligence toward the work of art which thereupon ceases to count as a

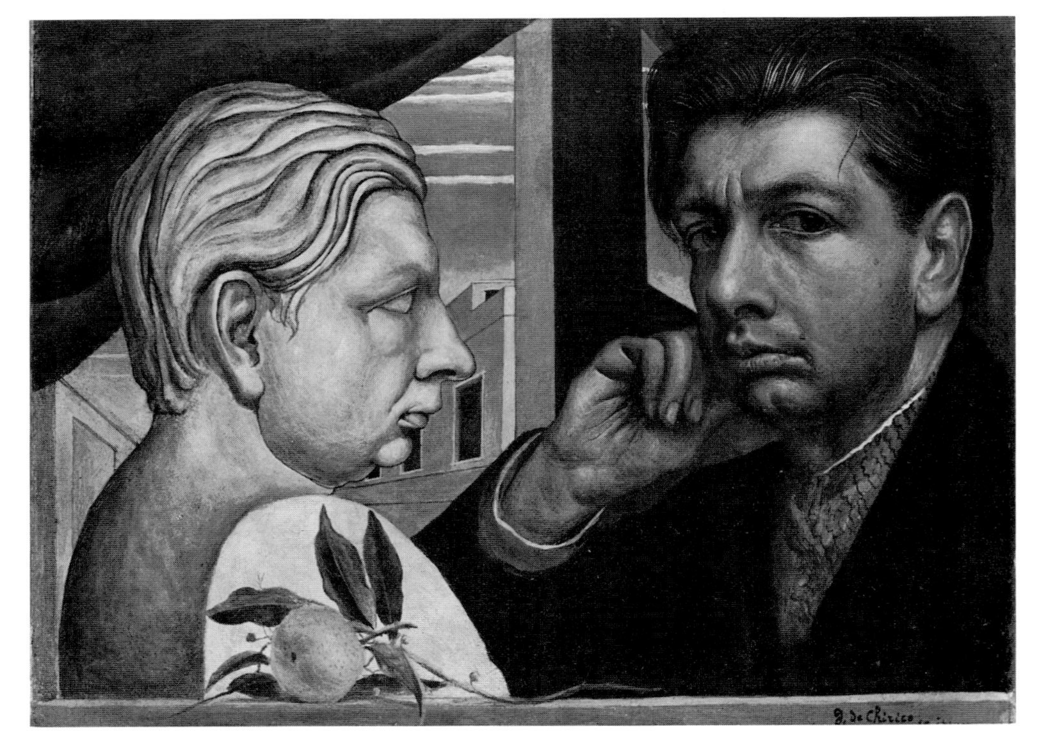

Fig. 26. Giorgio de Chirico, *Self-Portrait*, 1924. The Toledo Museum of Art, Toledo, Ohio. Gift of Edward Drummond Libbey

precious object, a marvel, a miracle, and is lowered to a level of mere artifice, more or less original, more or less qualified to satisfy the demands of connoisseurs of laundry and kitchen painting."[34] Because it lacks spiritual energy, Arcimboldesque naturalism took kitchen painting quite literally, at least to the extent that his portraits pivot on metaphorical transfers without any "hidden" depth. Whether casual or deliberate, form thrived on the "combinatory diversity" of Comanini's "*naturale e artificioso*" (*Trattati,* 3:254). Arcimboldo's manner of arranging details paved the way for surrealist dislocations. Both styles shared a double vision of the art object, which shows "two aspects: one current one which we see nearly always and which is seen by men in general, and the other which is spectral and metaphysical and is seen only by rare individuals in moments of clairvoyance."[35] In both instances, the object is and is not there. However self-effacing, the co-presence of similarity and dissimilarity is at once real and unreal.

In Surrealism, Ferdinand Alquié writes, the imaginary always strives "to break the framework of the given, to surpass it, to evoke an inaccessible to which the real itself must, nevertheless, be compared." The activity of fantastic imitation could be phrased in similar terms. Whereas the surrealists exploited metaphorical outreach to the point of "seizing the most feeble relation existing between objects taken at random,"[36] the mannerists were more logical in their choice of objects.

III

Double visions and improbable inventions edged at the periphery of Surrealism even before Arcimboldo and Comanini pitched fantasy against mimesis. At the very beginning of *On the Statue,* Alberti referred to "certain outlines" in tree trunks which, "through some light changes could be made to resemble a natural shape." For H. W. Janson, that was the first explicit statement linking artistic creation with images made by chance, a connection that has become a central aesthetic tenet of Dadaism and

Surrealism.[37] But it is in the treatise on painting that Alberti linked chance images to the grotesque: "Nature herself seems to delight in painting, for in the cut faces of marble she often paints centaurs" (*O.P.*, 67). At times, therefore, nature "delights" in replacing the mimetic with the unnatural. Delight, difficulty, and the grotesque are strung together in the Albertian treatise, which called attention to a potential aestheticism.

In the medium of painting, chance images have inspired artists through the ages. At the end of the fifteenth century, Leonardo da Vinci also noted that when "you look at a wall spotted with stains, or with a mixture of stones, if you have to devise some scene, you may discover a resemblance to strange faces and customs, and an endless variety of objects." Throughout the landscape of the arts, Mantegna's clouds (*nuvole*), Dürer's rocks, and stains on walls (*macchie*) called to mind artificial mixtures; fantasy thrived on randomness of inspiration. Thomas DaCosta Kaufmann has called attention to a letter in which Arcimboldo himself called grotesque decorations "*macchie*" (spots), the same word Leonardo had used to describe such a novel approach.[38]

IV

At the outer edges of *imitazione fantastica,* Comanini turned to a physical condition in which the mind's activity is basically visual:

> Poets write that Sleep has three ministers; Morpheus, who can transform himself in the features and manners of men; he imitates the voices, clothing, walk and language of each of them, even though he can only imitate men. Icelone, or Forbetera, who can turn into a beast, bird, snake, but not into men or any inanimate body. Fantaso, who represents only inanimate things to men, and transforms himself into earth, stone, wave, board, and other similar forms. If these were not fables, I would say that all three ministers of Sleep are very familiar to

> Arcimboldo, because he can perform all the acts and transformations that they do, since he can transform straws and vines into men and men's clothing, into women and women's clothing. (*Trattati,* 3:269–70)

Sleep can alter the order of reality at will. And it is on such grounds that the text turns to Arcimboldo's fantastic virtue, which made it possible for him to "make whatever he wanted—*ciò che vuole*" (ibid., 270). Dreams share with fantastic imitation a permutable activity that does not set forth a world-picture, but a picture of eccentricity in which knowledge is neither clear nor proportional.

Before Comanini, Leonardo da Vinci realized that sleep could bring abnormality within reach: "Man shall walk without moving, he shall speak with those who are absent, he shall hear those who do not speak." Although it uprooted the mechanisms of reality, sleep did not expand knowledge. In 1571, Giovan Battista Naldini linked his *Allegoria del Sogno* to the cycle of night and day. One moves toward the other through an enormous lens; like the lens, sleep deforms natural objects; by so doing it lays out a field of free investigation.[39]

Late in the sixteenth century, Jacopo Mazzoni rooted dreams and poetry in the power of fantasy. While resembling truth, they could "metaphorically be exchanged one for the other."[40] In the words of Arnold Hauser, who has studied analogical correspondences at the level of period concepts, "the nearest analogy to this world of mingled reality is the dream, in which real connections are abolished and things are brought into an abstract relationship to one another, but in which individual objects themselves are described with the greatest exactitude and the keenest fidelity to nature. It is, at the same time, reminiscent of contemporary art, as expressed in the description of associations in Surrealist art."[41] Throughout the arts, freedom could alter size, balance, and proportion to stupefying effects. And it was on the equally unreal grounds of fairy tales that literary figures such as Gilio, Lomazzo, and Tasso turned to monsters, while Battista Dossi painted lobster-soldiers.

Instead of leading toward the unknown, sleep fostered what

could be visible. Unreality and surreality became matters of either replacement or displacement in Comanini's treatise. Standing at bay of experience and objects of oneiric origin,[42] the artist derived methodological freedom from dreamlike states of mind. For the mannerists, thought preceded expression. The time was yet to come when artists would analyze sleep as a subconscious realm where unpremeditated metaphors could set off associations that reached Tristan Tzara's mouth and Alberto Savinio's fingertips automatically.

Comanini expected artists to "make" and "form" their images, since *capricci* were all but casual. They reduced reality to a thing, an *id,* made up of elements that could be mixed at will. At the surface, the mechanism of the puzzle and the mode of the grotesque juggled things without transforming them. For Breton, juxtapositions of the two terms of the surrealist metaphor are not conscious but fortuitous, because it is not within man's power to effect the clash of such distant realities.[43] At first Breton believed in interactions between reality and imagination. The second phase of Surrealism, however, threw poetic activity beyond the *déjà vu,* which Arcimboldo teased but never intended to dismiss altogether.

V

When Comanini wrote that *capricci* were to rest on their factual or presumed novelty ("*non più disegnato da alcun altro, almeno che gli sappia,* 256), he placed emphasis on knowledge of the artistic tradition, which took over mimesis in the realm of artifice. Like freaks vis-à-vis evolution, grotesque forms mark unique deviations from the historical flow. In that marginal position, Kafka shared with Ovid only a metamorphic approach to form, and one can find neither Bosch nor Vermeer in Dali.

From Arcimboldo to Dali, the grotesque so mastered the world of appearances that its *sur*real or *un*real details came to bear a striking resemblance to reality. Yet the mannerist could not foresee that the modern alliance between the grotesque and technology would make the marginal indistinguishable from the typical. Because it surrounds us everywhere, the grotesque has become increasingly invisible. Eccentricity at the margins has yielded to familiarity at the center, where recent criticism has placed the grotesque core of the poetics of transgression.[44]

In its mannerist and surrealist variants, imagination flaunted the realistic solidity of forms, which shaped an improbable world where the "given" made room for the marvelous. Beyond the *déjà vu*, the novelty of art was grounded on the ruins of what had been left behind.

Part II

Art That Reveals Art

5

The Unsightly Muselinda: Toward a Poetics of the Grotesque

For every sensible line of straightforward statement, there are leagues of senseless cacophonies, verbal jumbles and incoherences.
—Jorge Luis Borges

I

It was a mannerist project to make things "other" than natural. Excess therefore became predominant, and the mimesis of reality made room for inventions of the mind that were willfully antirepresentational. Eccentricity often replaced the natural with the grotesque.

While adding to Castiglione's praise of eclecticism in art, Erasmus's defense of variety at the beginning of the sixteenth century fell back on Horace, whose *Ars Poetica* takes on the grotesque at the very outset:

Humano capiti cervicem pictor equinam
iungere si velit, et varias inducere plumas
undique collatis membris, ut turpiter atrum
desinat in piscem mulier formosa superne,
spectatum admissi risum teneatis, amici?
credite, Pisones, isti tabulae fore librum
persimilem, cuius, uelut aegri somnia

(If a painter chose to join a human head to the neck of a horse, and to spread feathers of many a hue over limbs picked up now here now there, so that what at the top is a lovely woman ends below in a black and ugly fish, could you, my friends, if favoured with a private view, refrain from laughing? Believe me, dear Pisos, quite like such pictures would be a book, whose idle fancies shall be shaped like a sick man's dreams.)

A vocabulary of caprice, assemblage, unreality, and unorthodox unity turns away from mimesis. Horace's disruptive interlocutor claims the right of free expression (lines 9–10), but only to finger an artisan who, unlike true artists, is incapable of imparting "wholeness" ("*ponere totum*") to the parts (lines 38–40).[1]

Antiquity had tested mimesis through descriptions of hybrid centaurs and monstrous medleys from Virgil's *Aeneid* (iii) and Lucretius's *The Nature of the Universe* (iv) to the *Institutio Oratoria* (viii) of Quintilian. Even Socrates populated the world of the imagination with centaurs and Gorgons in *Phaedrus* (229c–d). For Vitruvius, the grotesque abused variety, courted unruly freedom, and produced "monsters rather than definite representations taken from definite things. . . . Such things neither are, nor can be, nor have been. . . . Yet, when people view these falsehoods, they approve rather than condemn" (*De Architectura* vii, 5).[2]

It is by now a fact that the "fantastic" Middle Ages rejoiced in the grotesque. To his dismay, Saint Bernard could not deny that Romanesque art valued "unnatural" inventions. Unwittingly, he coined the phrase *deformis formositas ac formosa deformitas*—"deformed beauty and beautiful deformity," which provided a

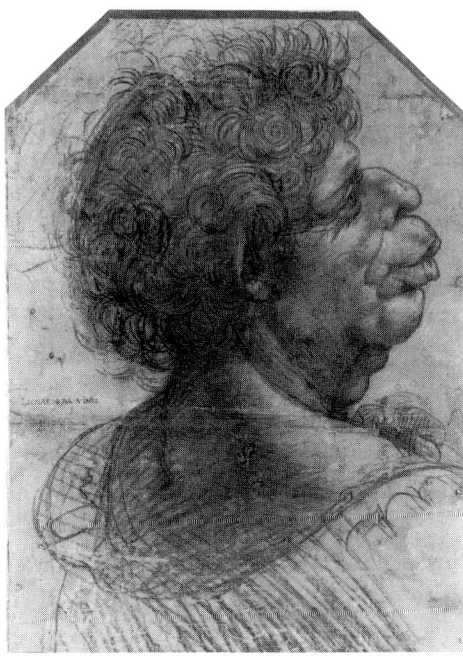

Fig. 27. Leonardo da Vinci, *Scaramuccia*, 1503–4. Christ Church Library, Oxford

nutshell definition for what was to govern much of mannerist painting, sculpture, and decoration from the Mantuan Palazzo del Tè to the gallery of Fontainebleau. Among the outstanding links in the development of the grotesque since the Middle Ages were Cennini, Doni, Leonardo da Vinci, Bosch, Dürer, and Vasari, who found Leonardo's head of Scaramuccia (1503–4; Fig. 27) very attractive. During the sixteenth century, some denounced the grotesque for lacking both *decorum* and symbolism; others defended it since it could yield "strange inventions" of a kind that "nature cannot do by itself"; and a few could tolerate that freedom only if applied to artworks placed in secular environments.[3] Eccentricity spawned abnormal attributes. Without a descriptive name, that style was christened by the humanists,[4] whose criticism of it actually took notice of its popularity.

However negative his approach to the grotesque, Horace

spelled out a procedure that shed light on the range of technique. On grotesque grounds, the excess of variety fostered unsightly fancies that would be upgraded into mannerist adumbrations. Likewise, the timid interlocutor of *Ars Poetica* became bold in the *Lives* of Vasari, whose emphasis on the interplay between *licenzia* and *regola* made room for stupefying forms of all kinds. As a measure of excess, variety infringed on unity in the morphology of mannerist eccentricity.

Aristotelian action and Albertian narrativity made selection crucial in matters of artistic unity, whose centripetal pull reversed itself in the world of the grotesque. Neither biological nor environmental laws could streamline form. Quantity became an index of quality, which often failed to find expression in the singular; function was resolved into accumulation. Architectural planes and pictorial spaces were crowded in a way analogous to that *maniera tedesca* that Alberti and Vasari detested.

It was a significant coincidence that the etymology of *grottesco* also refers to the topographical dislocation of the Domus Aurea, which was not meant to be underground at all. Although a mistake, the word did fit a style shy of the sunlit cosmos of classical and humanist architecture. The heavenly domes of the Pantheon in Rome and Santa Croce in Florence found their reverse in the Domus Aurea and the grottoes in the Boboli Gardens. Etymologically, *grotta* refers to *crupta,* which is a subterranean cell or cave. "Cryptical" also refers to something hidden or ambiguous, and cryptology points to enigmatic languages. Such a cluster of meanings described central attributes of the grotesque. The etymological mistake therefore was highly connotative amid a culture in need of a terminology as un-Apollonian as the Laocoön group unearthed in Rome at the turn of the sixteenth century.

II

To give focus to my analysis of the mannerist grotesque, Comanini's "*naturale et artificioso*" ought to be taken as a starting point. Whereas the natural is icastic, the artificial aims at producing forms that exist "only in the mind, and not outside of it" (*Trattati,* 3:254–55). The intellectual construct stands at the other side of nature, which is torn down and built up again in light of man-made criteria. The natural is a means, and the unnatural the end of grotesque art, which stems from epistemological eccentricity.

With an eye to size, excess has taken the form of hyperbole since the *Batrachomyomachia,* in which epic standards measure mock-heroic deeds of small animals. Within the tradition of medieval juxtapositions between enormity and minuteness, Isidore of Seville also thought of monsters—*makrobioi*—as either "a race standing twelve feet tall (in India)," or "a race with a stature of one cubit, whom the Greeks call Pygmies" (*Etymologiae* xi.3, 26–27).

When François I undertook the expansion of Fontainebleau, he paid equal attention to minute jewelry and grand architecture. Giambologna's Fountain of Neptune in Bologna has been called a "*soprammobile da piazza,*" and Cellini's *saliera* for Francesco I a "*monumento da tavola*" (Fig. 28). Two chapters of Cellini's *Trattato della scultura* deal with *colossi.* At the same time, rules are given for "*lavorare di minuteria*" in his *Trattato dell'oreficeria,* whose preface lauded Lorenzo Ghiberti for his "*opere piccole.*"

Large turtles at Bomarzo (Fig. 29) would carry small figures in the Boboli Gardens. In the wake of Pulci's oversize Morgante, Valerio Cioni created the fountain sculpture of Pietro Barbino, the *Dwarf Morgante—Morgante nano* (1600–1608; Fig. 30), a parodic miniaturization of the literary giant. As a dwarf, however, the figure is large: parody teases itself. Bronzino painted the same subject with a hunting owl, and Giambologna mounted it on a dragon. It is indeed revealing that Pulci's mock-epic is one that consciously set measure (*misura*) against mixture and excess (*miscuglio, quazzabuglio*):

> It is necessary here to go on the straight line
> (I do not know if it has gone too far)
> (*Morgante,* xxviii, 63)

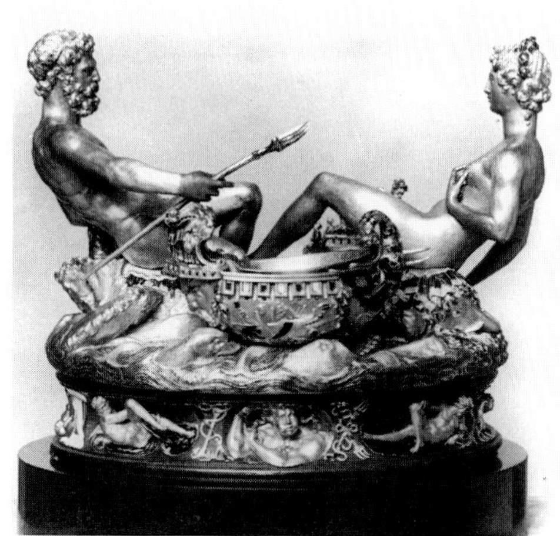

Fig. 28. Benvenuto Cellini, *Salt-Cellar,* 1540–43. Kunsthistorisches Museum, Vienna

Because action has run unchecked, proportion has given way to monstrous alterations of size, language, and invention.[5]

In architecture, a similar attitude carved small rooms for dwarfs in the majestic Palazzo Ducale at Mantua. There Pietro Barbino would have felt at ease. Michelangelo scaled down outdoor proportions to indoor size in the Laurentian Library (see Fig. 4), while the *studiolo* clashed with the monumentality of adjacent staterooms in Palazzo della Signoria. Linking architecture to geography, the *orti botanici* in Pisa and Florence lodged a miniature flora drawn from the ever-expanding boundaries of the known world. The *orto* was but a miniature effigy of a worldwide experience. In painting, subjects suitable for clashes of size were popular, from Battista Dossi's *Hercules and the Pygmies* and *The Blinding of Poliphemus* (1552; Fig. 31) by Pellegrino Tebaldi to the giants of Giulio Romano and the colossus of Rhodes by Martin van Heemskerck. Like *perfezione,* proportion had to "outdo" itself either by defect or excess.

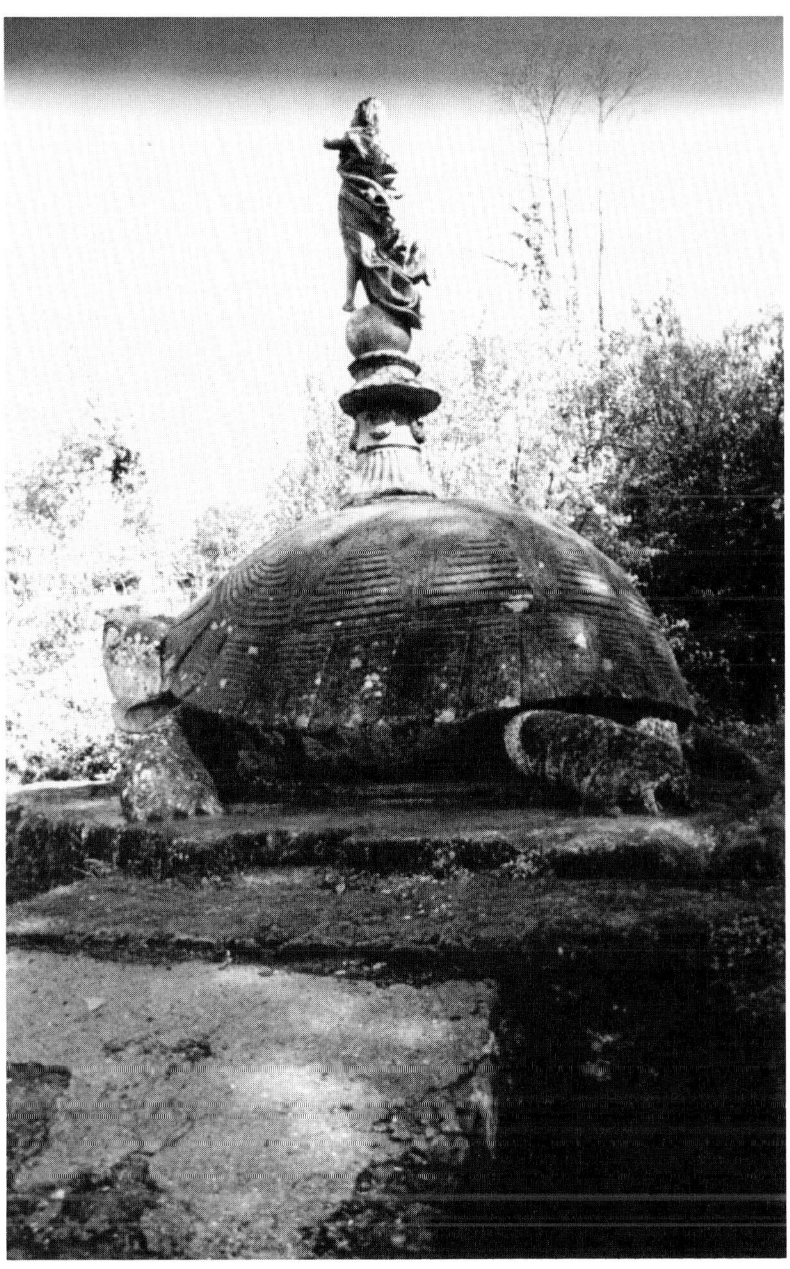

Fig. 29. Giant Turtle. Bosco sacro, Bomarzo

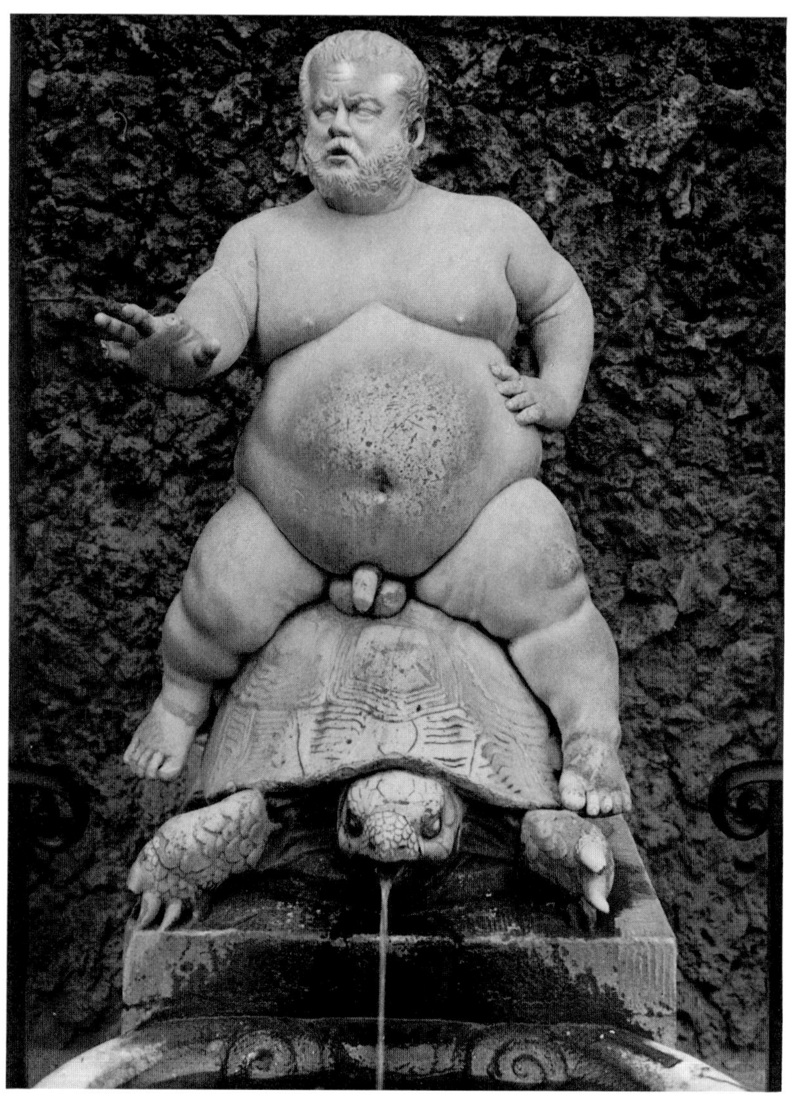

Fig. 30. Valerio Cioni, *Fountain of the Dwarf Morgante*, 1600–1608. Boboli Gardens, Florence

Without adding to the world of knowledge, even language widened its range. The very etymology of *monstrum* refers to anomalous birth, defect of nature, and something outside the known order. In nature, the crossing of a horse with a donkey generates the mule, which is sterile. Likewise, hermaphrodites and monsters subvert the order of nature in Ovidian literature.

In the world of literary fictions, inversions of size violated the rhetorical sequence of discourse, which yielded tall tales and linguistic exaggerations in Rabelaisian narratives. Pantagruel and Panurge, in fact, honored the virtues of the foolish Triboulet in three pages of a double-column list of attributes in *Gargantua and Pantagruel* (III, 38). Grotesque forms "had" to transgress the figurative lifelike; as a result, the unlifelike had to be either bigger or smaller than lifesize. We ought to agree with Susan Stewart that miniature favors "diminutive" versions of experience that are essentially spatial.[6] The same holds true in the case of its opposite: gigantism.

As a figure of visual abnormality, the grotesque fed on a heterogeneous culture familiar with Erasmian folly, Brant's ship of fools, and artforms that steered religion toward the monstrous worlds of Bosch and Bruegel, whose *The Tower of Babel* (1563) stood as an icon of visual excess and linguistic disorientation. Whereas it remained either moral or political in northern European art, the grotesque leaned toward playfulness along Mediterranean shores. Children and childish adults in Bruegel's *Children's Games* (1560) would have roamed with ease in the Italian villas at Bomarzo, Bagnaia, and Pratolino. On either side of the Alps, the grotesque transgressed the logic of categorical and mimetic concepts, much as tautology meddled with the economy of language.

At the margins of *docere,* a ludic autonomy courted the grotesque, whose liminality Geoffrey Harpham has linked to the paintings of Arcimboldo. In a canvas such as *The Water* (see Fig. 8), we see fish close by and a human face at a distance. In between, confusion sets in; identity is split and referentiality spawns uncertain choices. Art is lodged between two worlds, where vision and ontology become grotesque insofar as they

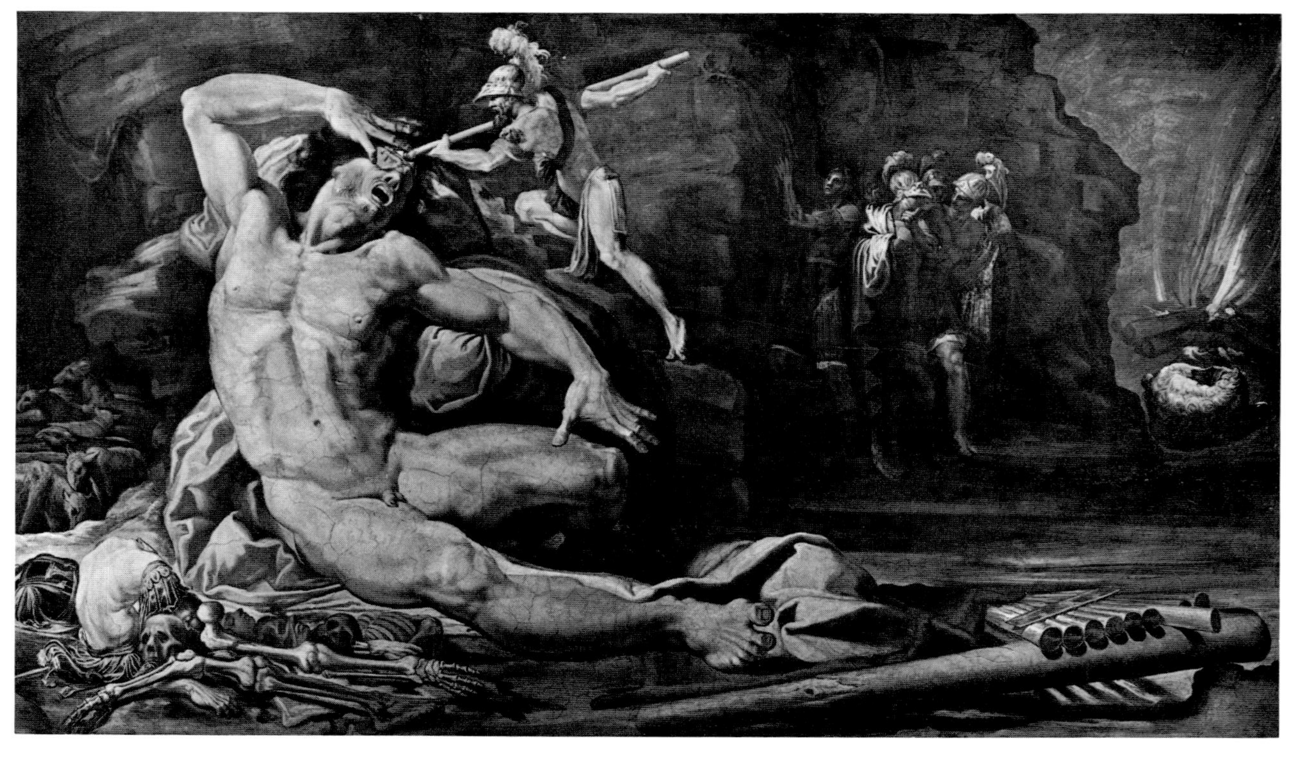

Fig. 31. Pellegrino Tebaldi, *The Blinding of Poliphemus*. Palazzo Poggi, Bologna

justify "multiple and mutually exclusive interpretations" that tease normality and abnormality.[7]

If anywhere, the grotesque prospers at the outer reaches of liminality; not between art and life but between art and artificiality. I would suggest that the empirical stands to the liminal as the figurative stands to the grotesque, which is an anomaly within a system thrown to the other side of the world of mimesis. The grotesque is not a way station in which the formless awaits to be "formed," but an ambivalent mechanism out to mix the text of nature with that of culture.

Especially in its mannerist disguise, eccentricity turns on itself; because it is ex-centric, it moves away, around, and about the center. In a merrymaking mode, the grotesque feeds on antiacademism and scorns the confrontational freedom of any "neo-anti-counter." Looking as it does for marginality, the grotesque tests neither hierarchies of merit nor prevalent ideologies. Instead, it settles midway between norm and antinorm, same and other. At the outermost periphery of Mannerism, *proporzione* and *sprezzatura* became *artificiose* for Comanini, and it is there that *perfezione* became *somma, maravigliosa,* and *molto più assoluta* for Vasari.

III

Since it would be unwelcomed on Parnassus, where and under what conditions would the unsightly muse of the grotesque feel at ease? G. P. Lomazzo offered a clue when he wrote poems in the grotesque mode, which he tied to the alliance between the natural and the bizarre. As such,

> Il grottesco non meno anche vale
> quando in far una cosa un'altra prende.
> Quindi i concetti son si oscuri e chiari
> ch'usciti paion fuor dal gran caosse.

> (The grotesque is not any less valuable
> when it takes one thing to make another.
> Therefore its concepts are so obscure and clear
> That they seem to have come out of chaos.)
> (*Rime ad imitazione di grotteschi* [Milan, 1587])

Mannerist dissimulation finds its roots in chaos, whose heterogeneous nature shelters paradox, antitheses, and unreality. Whereas cosmos rests with the proportional order of beauty, chaos thrives on clashes between beauty and ugliness, thus opening the door to a plurality of standards.

Short of unruly disorder, however, chaos dislocated proportion, which Vincenzo Danti linked to artifice under the aegis of *proporzione artificiosa:* "The proportion of unequal things will be ever more artificial and will produce a greater beauty than that stemming from similar things" (*Trattati,* 1:234). Like Arcimboldo, Lomazzo cherished alterations of natural forms: "*Nasce il bizar grotesco . . . dal naturale.*"[8] The mimetic had to make room for the artificial. Literary and pictorial grotesques therefore shared unspatial and enigmatic attributes. Growth was denied and ornament became structural. Because it is incompatible with any notion of process, the grotesque can only be a construct. Form became intransitive.[9]

On grotesque grounds, language lost hold of narration amid the discontinuity of an artificial world that was overwhelmingly visual. A case in point, Comanini's poem on Arcimboldo's *Vertumnus* can comment on the grotesque only through the rejection of meaning as knowledge. Repetition of words and rhetorical questions tease the possibility of substantive statements. Much as it impairs figurative realism, the image also blurs the syntax of a literary discourse that could double itself on the chessboard of art. A wedge was deepening between the philosophy of things (*res*) and the rhetoric of words (*verba*), which began to carve an autonomous realm in which mannerist invention was set free. Since it had to stir emotions, art mixed the icastic with the prodigious, and the outcome often was grotesque.[10]

In the grotesque mode, art neither confronts nor denies matters of epistemology. Michel Foucault has found in Magritte's "nonaffirmative verbal statements" an intransitive concept of art akin to the mannerist experience.[11] Beyond the restrictions that autonomy places on any form of expression, *imitazione fantastica* found in the grotesque a key that opened the door to an eccentric world of marvels.

IV

To outline the poetics of the grotesque, I shall at this point pull together its character, form, and language. Machiavelli had no problems in calling on the ancient centaur as a teacher of heroes in *The Prince,* for the mythic hybrid spoke a human language. Within the mannerist experience, centaurs and harpies give out animallike and bodylike sounds that range from *latrare* and *fischiare* to *sibilare* and *vomitare* in Tasso's *Gerusalemme liberata* (iv, 5). However repulsive, grotesque utterances of that sort found their way into the transitive discourse of human experience.

Yet the world of Homeric cyclops had no laws; they did not till the land, and their denial of traditional modes of life affected even the civilized language of Ulysses, who identified himself as Nobody-Noman in their midst (*Odyssey* ix). And when Isidore of Seville wrote his *Etymologiae* in the seventh century A.D., monsters and cyclops were "said to be without tongues, using nods and motions to speak with each other" (xi.3.18). Logic tells us that hybrid races should speak hybrid languages. Everything ought to be abnormal in the world of unnatural exaggeration: more or less than linguistic, and more or less than lifesize at the other side of any standard of normality.

Geographical traditions placed "the other side" at the periphery of the Mediterranean world, where harmony was lost to dissonance and proportion to disproportion. Because it reenacted lost grandeur and superhuman bliss in antiquity, hyperbole was meant to reconcile microcosm with macrocosm, myth with history, and humanity with divinity. Yet Aristotelianism saw in "excess and deficiency" marks of vice, whereas observance of the mean was a "mark of virtue" (*The Nicomachean Ethics* 2.6.5.9–14).

The excellence of the mean—which measured the very core of virtue—was set at the geographical center of the Greco-Roman world. So framed, the "grotesque" opening of Horace's *Ars Poetica* set off a blunt defense of the "mean" against unproportional monstrosities of all kinds. The proportional center held, but ex-centric pulls were being felt; decor stood vis-à-vis hyperbole, that is to say, lack of fitness.

At the periphery of culture, virtue would turn into vice, proportion into extravagance, and the economy of the Attic style into Asiatic redundancy. Away from the center, one would meet barbarians, savages, wild men, and monstrous races. "Extremes of form and places," John B. Friedman reminds us, "were closely linked in antiquity and the Middle Ages. . . . the very greatest extreme was assumed to exist beyond the borders of the known, and held a great fascination for the observer at the center."[12]

Since antiquity, hybrids have been vehicles for the grotesque. From the world of myth to Mantegna's *Minerva Expelling the Vices from the Garden of Virtue* (1496–97), satyrs acted out the sexual excess of satyriasis and nymphomania. Marsyas's immoderate pride was brutally punished by Apollo, and the old Silenus could speak words of wisdom only when wine loosened his tongue. The Italian tradition updated the classical heritage. Standing by Venus and Bacchus with apelike faces, satyrs turned love and fertility into vice and lust. They all led lives outside social constraints. Their wind instruments—flute and syrinx—stirred passions to the exclusion of the rational appeal of speech, which would be accompanied by strings.

Since this chapter focuses on poetics, we ought to take notice of William Hazlitt's reference to Pan in his discussion of romantic excess: "Our literature, in a word, is Gothic and grotesque; unequal and irregular. . . . It aims at an excess of beauty or power. . . . Perhaps, the genius of our poetry has more of Pan than of Apollo." Etymologically, Pan means "everything." The god is an all-encompassing hybrid; everything could easily edge on "too much." And so it happened that mannerist and romantic appraisals of the deity underlined the irregular character of what Nietzsche considered the "titanic" pride of Dionysian "excess."[13]

Granted that common sense is either irrelevant or paradoxical on matters of the grotesque, attempts at finding a language congenial with its intransitive nature must dismiss anarchic freedom from established codes. For certain, the grotesque is neither naive nor unruly, and its language responds to eccentricity for its own sake. Unlike Isidore of Seville, who still concerned himself with the relationship between names and things, Abelard pinned etymology on the words themselves. For him, the universe was neither a thing nor an idea, but a world of words that produced experimentation with antilanguage (Guillaume le Vivier, Villon, Rutebeuf) and unruly poetry (Marot, Baudouin de Conde). Their "possible" and "impossible" *fatras* could be alingual, as in the case of Guillaume d'Aquitaine's *Dodododo Dodododo dododo dodelle,* and bilingual, as in the case of Watriguet de Couvin's *Ave, douz non de Maria / Marie en cui Diex maria.*

At this point, we ought to pause on the ingrained correlation between excess, abnormality, and the grotesque. On matters of historical extravagance, Isidore of Seville linked a race of men having two rows of teeth, the Cynodontes, to a discussion of superfluity (*Etymologiae* 3.7). Too many teeth and too many tongues—not to mention Aristotelian creatures with extra feet and heads as exceptions to "generic types" (*Generation of Animals*)—therefore begin to add up to an anatomy suitable for the superfluity of hyperboles and tautologies, as well as for the abnormality of the grotesque.

In the midst of the humanist experience, such a correlation surfaced again in as apparently an unrelated subject as Poggio Bracciolini's treatise *On Avarice* (1428–29). Even on the subject of wealth and its distribution, sufficiency and moderation must be the norm. At its polar extremes, one finds the deplorable excess of "avarice and lust," the latter being an evil vector of prodigality and luxury. References to Virgil center on monstrous creatures such as Furies and Harpies, whereas a quotation from Saint John Chrysostom leads to "monstrous architects," that is to say, greedy men who infest the city.[14] As a sustained form of classical infraction, such a monstrous lack of measure spawned images of grotesque distortions.

If one tried to guess what language modern sixteenth-century giants might speak "as giants," we would have to turn to the Rabelaisian "*galerie de tableaux grotesques*" in *Gargantua and Pantagruel* (1532–53). After exposure to the "*langaige diabolique*" and "*la rédundance litinicome*" of a Limousin who mangled French (II, 6), Pantagruel came across Panurge's strange compounds of fantastic and grotesque mixtures such as "*jocststzampenards,*" "*delmeupplist rincq,*" an Anglo-French term meaning "*donne-moi please-to-drink*"). Throughout the book, one finds "*des mots hybrides, richement métisses, des hippocampelephantocamelos linguistique.*"[15] Yet it is Panurge—"a tall, handsome chap who was physically very well set up" (II, 9)— that speaks a grotesque jargon; the giants do not. The grotesque may appear to be primitive, but it is not.

Later in the book, Rabelaïs describes a world without debtors and borrowers; yet, lack of tensions has muted the activities of life. At that point, the earth would "produce nothing but Monsters, Titans, Aloidae, and Giants. Rains will not rain, light will not shine . . . Lucifer will break loose . . . men will be wolves in the form of men, werewolves and goblins" (III, 3). But the nagging question does not let up; what language would they speak in that intransitive state of affairs? What we do know is that Rabelais's *gigantisme verbal* could not dispense with the operative reality of Gargantua and Pantagruel.

A more interesting case is the grotesque anatomy of *Quaresmeprenant*-Lentkeeper (IV, 31–32), an Arcimboldesque monster whose internal and external organs Rabelais describes through a mesmerizing wealth of similies:

> A beard like a lantern
> A chin like a pumpkin
> Ears like a pair of mittens
> . . . .
> If he spit, it was baskets of artichokes;
> If he blew his nose, it was salted eels.

Such an anatomical composite is not functional: "He worked at doing nothing and did nothing when he worked . . . he ate nothing fasting and fasted doing nothing." In a mode by now familiar to us, language spells inanity; yet, it sustains a state of idleness in which the text emphasizes description instead of scripture. The subject becomes object; verbs of activity such as "work" and "do" halt movement and deny each other; enumeration feeds on itself; and syntax is broken down into words that become icastic objects, before reappearing in the guise of visually frozen—*dégelées*—voices (IV, 55).

By denying speech to the giant, Rabelais denies him the possibility of entering the discourse of life. Because absence of language stemmed from a world upside down, one could expect Lentkeeper to dry "himself in ponds and rivers" and fish "in the air." And we cannot be surprised if his throat was "like a lump of tow" inside and "like a hippocras-filter" outside. When he spoke, "it was heavy sack cloth from Auvergne, so far was it from being that bright-colored silk, of which Parysatis wished to have woven to words of those who spoke to her son, Cyrus, king of the Persians." Common language, or distortions thereof, proved inadequate to carry a grotesque speech that was never spelled out. Since he coughed "boxes of marmalade" and sneezed "barrels of mustard," could he utter anything other than grotesque lumps? At that point, irregularity and eccentricity could shape themselves into a physical morphology. In the deformed realm of Antiphysis, Lentkeeper could thrive only on the hybrid language of *vocables fantaisistes* and *mots-centaures*, that is to say, a verbal pastiche.

In the mode of eccentricity, we ought to expect an abnormal language from gullets "like a grape-basket." Among animals in the faraway land of Satin, Panurge found leucrocutes with the "mouth up to the ears" who "speak with human voices, but when they do, they say nothing." On the other hand, manticores have "three rows of teeth" and "a very melodious voice." Hearsay is "a diminutive, monstrous, mis-shapen old fellow. . . . His mouth was slit up to his ears, and in it were seven tongues, each of them cleft into seven parts. However he chattered, tattled, and prated with all the seven at once, of different matters, and in divers languages" (V, 30–31). Perhaps Christopher Columbus was waiting to hear a language of that sort amid those monstrous races that the ancients had located in India and the Italian navigator never found on the new "Indian" shores.

In his unmatched essays on Marco Polo and the Marvels of the East, Rudolph Wittkower reminds us that Aldo Manutius published classical texts as well as prophetic treatises based on the appearance of monsters in Europe. It was in the sixteenth century that the systematic study of monstrosities led to the creation of teratology.[16]

In his analysis of linguistic experiments at the turn of the sixteenth century, Mario Praz has found an ancestor of Mannerism in Francesco Colonna, a Joyce of the *Quattrocento* whose *Hypnerotomachia Poliphili* is crowded with hybrids of Italian, Latin, Greek, and macaronic unheard of before or since. His text indulges in a grammar of ornament mixing vernaculars with ancient inscriptions. One can guess that such a language could have been written, if anywhere, in the tomes making up Arcimboldo's *Librarian*. And it is possible that those books would contain a verbal hodgepodge in which definition has given way to glosses on words with contradictory meanings.[17] Within the grotesque framework, language became a field of lexical anamorphoses.

To a significant extent, meaning exhausted its potential, and Anton Francesco Doni so phrased the shift from the truth of discourse to the delights of dissimulation: "What happens today already has happened before; what is said now has been said and will be said again; what is going to be has taken place." If we were to find a mannerist place of work for *The Librarian*, Doni would welcome him in the colossal Babel of his *Libraria* (1550), where entries on nonsense in books never finished would not offend an illiterate public. Much like the pictorial grotesque, writing spells out permutations of alphabetical letters on pages whose headings are "a grammatical struggle"—"*la zuffa della grammatica*" and "a loot of words"—"*il bottino di vocaboli.*" Books would be found to contain a deluge of words—"*diluvio di parole*"—apt to produce ever-new combinations without falling outside the alphabet—"*pur non s'esce dall'alfabeto.*" Like the forms of language they stored, mannerist libraries were labyrinths of errors—"*laberinto d'errori*"—in which words grew on other words amid a plethora of printed authors—"*autori stampati.*" Rewriting and falsification triumphed. Reality itself came to be viewed as an alphabetical world that could disregard truth altogether.[18] If one were to open some of the older volumes in Arcimboldo's *Librarian* under the aegis of mannerist contextuality, he could find linguistic enigmas meant to confuse the keenest eyes, as it was the case with Marot's *poème-rebus,* and gamelike instructions for the teaching of grammar and logic in Mathias Ringmann's *Grammatica figurata,* Lefèvre d'Etaples's *Rhytmomachia,* and Thomas Murner's *Chartiludium logicae.*

Neologisms flourished, and Rabelais created words dozens of letters long that paved the way for Joyce's opening one-hundred-letter thunderclap in *Finnegans Wake.* Since *langage* cannot be pronounced, *écriture* bears on the visual character of consonants that are meant to fail meaning as well as reading. One can utter "hymptyhillhead" but cannot chant a one-hundred-letter thunderclap.[19] We thus confront a portmanteau vocabulary of excess edging on language as performance rather than as communication. In the realm of the grotesque, etymology is not a matter of roots but of transplants, parodic overgrowth, and parasitic accumulations.

Such linguistic vice versas were to become familiar to Samuel Beckett's Watt, who "took it into his head to invert, no longer the order of words in the sentence, nor that of the letters in the word, nor that of the sentences in the period,"[20] but to reverse all of them at the same time. It is indeed relevant that many of Beckett's figures bear monstrous traits, from Miss Dew's duck's disease to the anthropoid character of Miss Counihan. Yet modern connections between pathology and grotesqueness are extreme vis-à-vis the more festive experiments of Edward Lear in *The Yonghy Bonghy-Bo,* Lewis Carroll's nonsense language of Wonderland, and Alfred Jarry's pataphysics. To eccentricity's delight, all such languages have no consistent word-meaning correspondences; they playfully worded the science of nonsense.[21]

V

If one were to visualize the grotesque muse, it would be a bifront figure whose anamorphic sight could turn oblique looks toward both imitation and invention. Beyond the world of myth, she has kept custody over man's struggle to outdo nature and break free of the pulse of life. Like Circe, she lures the artist into a hedonistic world where there is no death because there was no life to begin with. Instead of turning men into swine, she would demand that art bring metamorphosis to a standstill so that artifice could conquer all worlds. And if one had to draw the features of that enchantress, her model could as well be one of Arcimboldo's portraits.

To be herself, the parasitic muse must deform another language. To enforce that, the *maniera arcimboldesca* and the *tradizioni petrarchesche, bernesche,* and *bembesche* were readily at hand. They provided the grammar and dictionary for tropes of repetition. A whole spectrum of commentaries, expositions, lessons, and imitations let the mind indulge in "*isti,*" "*ismi,*" and "*eschi*" that glossed matter into manner.[22] It was typically mannerist "to wit the reflexive, learned consciousness of the purely formal and aesthetic values in one's own and others' poetry."[23] And one need only turn to Lomazzo's *bizar grottesco* and Doni's antiliterary *La Zucca* and *La Pittura* (1565) to weigh mannerist leanings that became untranslatable in the following stanza:

> Tristizie, filastroccole, chimere,
> Viluppi, fanfalucole, proverbi,
> Leggende, ciance, pappolate, e verbi.[24]

We confront here a playful syntax of unmeaning. Writing in the grotesque mode triumphed wherever knowledge yielded to the centrifugal pull of incongruity.[25]

At this point, a question ought to be raised: What language does, or would, the grotesque muse speak? The immediate answer is that it might dissimulate rhetoric and spontaneity alike.

At first she should dislocate language into a composite "other" of no functional usage.

Within the domain of Castiglione's playful aestheticism, the subject of laughter leads to a discussion of verbal puns, which are anchored to deformity, incongruity, ambiguity, marvel, and the unexpected: indeed, the eccentric fabric of the grotesque. One pun goes as follows: "When the other day there was a discussion about making a fine brick floor (*un bel mattonato*) in the Duchess's room, and after much talk, you, Giancristoforo, said: 'If we could take the Bishop of Potenza and have him well flattened out, it would be much to the purpose, because he is the craziest man born (*il piu bel matto nato*).' Everyone laughed much, for by dividing the word *mattonato* you made the pun" (157–58). Separation and conjunction change the meaning of words; the thing becomes a person, and vice versa.

Against such a background, Lionardo Salviati distorted Tasso's language: "*Checcanuto, ordegni, tendindi, mantremante, impastacani . . . crinchincima.*" Two or more words are enmeshed into compounds that fail to make sense. The functionally contiguous *che canuto* becomes grotesquely continuous: *checcanuto*. And so does *man tremante* and *crin ch'in cima*, which become *mantremante* and *crinchincima*. Such verbal hybrids change euphony into cacophony and clarity into visual disarray. Yet, if one stops to analyze and dissect, some sense can be drawn out, since we can visually separate the original words, or details thereof, through a process also familiar to readers of *Ulysses* and *Finnegans Wake*.[26] From Rabelais and Salviati to Joyce and Leiris, the modern writer seems to have taken seriously Aristotle's statement about compound words: "A new coinage is a word used by the poet but by no one else" (*Poetics* 21).

Actually, the grotesque would enforce what Aristotle warned against. At first it is desirable that one look for "unusual words," for they "give dignity to the language and avoid colloquialism . . . for men admire what is remote, and that which excites admiration is pleasant" (*Rhetoric* 1404b). However, "all one's language" should not consist of "metaphors, lengthened forms, anything contrary to current usage," because the result would be either "riddle or a piece of barbarism; riddle if made up of metaphors, barbarism if made up of foreign words" (*Poetics* 22).

Even better than Aristotle, Quintilian foresaw the possibility that rhetoric could foster the creation of an autonomous world of linguistic forms:

> The usual result of over-attention to the niceties of style is the deterioration of our eloquence. The main reason for this is that those words are best which are least far-fetched and give the impression of simplicity and reality. For those words which are obviously the result of careful search and even seem to parade their self-conscious art, fail to attain the grace at which they aim and lose all appearance of sincerity because they darken the sense and choke the good seed by their own luxuriant overgrowth. For in our passion for words we paraphrase what might be said in plain language, repeat what we have already said at sufficient length, pile up a number of words where one would suffice; and regard allusion as better than directness of speech. (*Institutio Oratoria* viii, 23–24)

That point was reached when art turned from the language of human commerce to that of art alone. Quintilian warned us to "bear in mind that nothing should be done for the sake of words only, since words were invented merely to give expression to things" (viii, 32). The moment came when words uttered other words.

Among "modern" sinners against language, the mannerists would confess to tautological abuses. Logology—which preserved the metaphysical clarity of knowledge free of linguistic inadequacies—thus degenerated into logomachy, which dictionaries define as a dispute about words, a war of words having little or no actual contact with reality. For Kenneth Burke, logomachy toys with unity and separation inasmuch as it relies on "stylistic subterfuges for presenting real divisions in terms that deny division." To share such a "fallen" experience of art, readers must find a criticial standpoint where logomachy reveals both distortion and correction. At the mannerist threshold, anamorphosis and tautology put forth a grotesque metalanguage that could have reminded Burke of his own "speech-of-speeches," above "the single speeches,"

> And above this
> A Speech-of-speech-of-speeches
> (*Dialectician's Prayer*)

At that juncture, incongruity cut into the grotesque, which Burke defined as a "perception of discordances" on the strength, or under the spell, of which Joyce first blasted the verbal atoms of meaning apart and then used its remains to produce linguistic gargoyles.[27]

VI

I would like to think that the grotesque muse was born on a Mardi Gras after Babel somewhere around the island of Crete.[28] There she took up the suffix *linda,* which in Greek refers to children's games. To be true to the playful indirections of her mystifying appearance, she has stood mockingly within sight of her Parnassian cohorts.

While courting what could be said otherwise, Muselinda would agree with Jorge Luis Borges that, in the labyrinth,[29] it would make sense to speak "a Samoyedic Lithuanian dialect of Guarani, with classical Arabian inflections" (*The Library of Babel*). Amid written texts, she would crown Giovanni de' Rinaldi's *Il Mostruosissimo Mostro* (1588), which equated the book with the deformed birth of a most monstrous monster—*questo mio abortivo parto, se bene mostruoso* (preface). On her recommendation, it would indeed be proper to find relief and pleasure in readings of that sort. Furthermore, she would agree wholeheartedly with the modern critic that "the effect of etymological retracing is not to ground the word solidly but to render it unstable, equivocal, wavering." Backward displacements of that kind would render the very idea of the Source ex-centric. In fact, "all etymology is false etymology."[30] While she could open her eyes only beyond the *déjà vu*, her jumbled voice would untune the *déjà dit*.

As a grotesque figure, Muselinda is a dislocated deity who would feel right at home on the artificial Monte Parnasso in Villa Demidoff at Pratolino as well as in the halls of Fontainebleau.[31] There she would dispense "pragmatic holidays" for unspelling the science of *metaphorology*.[32] In the figurative guise of an Arcimboldesque face taking pleasure in her Rabelaisian carnival of verbality,[33] the unsightly deity could not be completely herself, but as a she-*id* adumbrating flowers of speech on the artful scoreboard of unfathomable marvels.

Conclusion

6

Homo Rhetoricus: The Daedalian Punster

What kind of man would homo rhetoricus *be? Rhetorical man is trained not to discover reality but to manipulate it. . . . Rhetorical man will always be an unregenerate punster.*

—Richard Lanham

I

Since antiquity, the grotesque has been part of art and mythology. As a hybrid monster with the body of a man and the head of a bull, the Minotaur lived in a labyrinth that Daedalus built on the island of Crete. The multitalented architect could set in stone

> Confusion and conflict, and deceive the eye
> With devious aisles and passages.

In the Ovidian narration, he eventually

turned his thinking
Toward unknown arts, changing the laws of nature
(*Metamorphoses* viii)

Leonardo would have been lured by thoughts of that kind as much as eclectic peers in Prague and Florence, from Arcimboldo to Buontalenti.

Daedalus had to build himself up into a birdlike machine to leave the labyrinth. The moment he lifted off he became birdlike for people on earth; even though he exceeded all of them, his condition was metaphorically unbirdly, ungodly, and inhuman. In the Ovidian text, Leonard Barkan writes, Daedalus defied the order he wanted to imitate by the act of imitation itself.[1] In Crete, the naturelike Minotaur and the machinelike Daedalus mixed grotesque features; both of them courted abnormality.

II

For a better understanding of mannerist transgressions, it would be helpful to focus on the mythic role played by the maze-maker. To satisfy Pasiphaë's forbidden desire, Daedalus built a wooden cow; she hid in it and coupled with the magnificent bull that Minos refused to kill in honor of Poseidon. The offspring was a monster that exacted human lives every nine years. The Daedalian trick backfired. Human make-believe deceived nature. Through cunning, Daedalus made bull-like and bird-like artifacts that looked natural. Their aesthetic affiliation was undoubtedly mannerist, even though the mythic outcome was not ludic at all.

Another Greek islander, named Ulysses, may have remembered the Daedalian feat when he built a larger wooden horse to deceive the Trojans and cause greater loss of life. During the age of Renaissance inventions, Leonardo da Vinci planned to hide men and firepower in a wooden crate that no longer looked like a horse. Posterity would call it a tank, and its deadly power was finally unleashed the world over. If the discourse of historical progress yielded such forms of devastation, was there any reason to get out of the maze? Who was the greater monster: the Minotaur or Daedalus trying to escape from Crete in a birdlike shape?

Once myth left Cretan shores, the Minotaur found refuge at the margins of literary and visual representations. To survive, the mannerist Minotaur did not need to consume the bloody flesh of historical experiences. Instead, the forms of art alone could make his existence autonomous. Whereas Ovidian creatures were capable of changing into other forms without restraints, the Minotaur could be neither an animal nor a man, but only a composite of both.[2] The Protean matter of mythology had exhausted much of its resilience by the time Minos offended Poseidon by replacing the bull he offered him.

The gods were losing their grip on mankind, and Daedalian pride was beginning to create mythologies of its own. In a way, the Minotaur, and any other mannerist descendant of his, was a product of that challenge. He knew that his position was subordinate and learned to live with his unique nature. On the subject of hybrids, Machiavelli tells us that "Achilles and many other ancient princes were given to Chiron the Centaur to be raised and taught under his discipline. This can only mean that, having a half-beast and half-man as a teacher, a prince must know how to employ the nature of the one and the other" (*The Prince,* xviii). Chiron was a figure of synthesis; through him, myth enlightened history. The Minotaur instead is a figure of division. He was killed, but the maze survived him; myth severed itself from history. The cobweb outlasted the spider. Parasitic as it always had been, the mannerist spider then moved in. In the locus of hybrid dividedness, he was the "other" spider that would endure, the "other" Minotaur who would not pretend to take up educational projects. In an Arcimboldesque guise, he only wanted to tease and entertain outside the provinces of both need and ideas.

The mannerist Minotaur would be interested in neither threads nor waxen wings. Instead, he would make fun of his own story and of his own nature, as well as all other stories and everyone else's nature. His divided self could manipulate only forms of division. After all, reputable Minotaurs live on islands off the mainland, and their mazes are there to make separation even more tangible.

Pierre Vidal-Naquet would suggest that the Minotaur's hybrid dividedness was Daedalus's own.[3] Ancient writers called him either "the Athenian" or "the Cretan." Duplicity affected origin and identity. To date, two or three sets of parents have been put forward.[4] In light of that genealogy, it could be expected of him to double into a birdlike "other." Myth tells us that our double is the statue, and Daedalus was the sculptor who made his statues walk. One of them was a gigantic automaton that stood guard over the island by spitting fire from its mouth. Its name was Talos, but Talos also was the name of Daedalus's nephew, the young sculptor killed by his envious uncle on the mainland. The Daedalian experience was one that just kept doubling up.

III

What happened in mythology happened again to Western cultures after the dawn of history. When a civilization begins to decline, there is always some smart Daedalus who gives up flying once he has run out of winged ideas that could engage mind and body. He thus starts to toy with his own ingenuity. And while others would submit to fate, he just cannot let his talent go to waste. Yet the lifestream of progress outside the maze is too much for him to take, nor could he forget that it already had taken his son's life.

It is at cultural junctures of that sort that Minotaurs often appear, beginning to tell tall tales about Daedalian eccentricity. On matters of ideological content, the mannerist Minotaur puts the maze to use, he does not build it. Metaphorically, therefore, he does not create language either. He assumes that everything already has been said and that all books have been written. It is his task to make up hybrid words as well as images more or less representative of his own discordant nature. Probably the Minotaur would mispronounce Daedalus's name as well as anyone else's language. Homer reminds us that Daedalus also built a dance floor for Ariadne (*Iliad* xviii). The maze might have been built on that spot, and rumor has it that Daedalus choreographed an artistic performance for it.

The thread of Ariadne is a narrative line that led Theseus to use and abuse Ariadne herself. However tragic, the thread unraveled the mythic story. From the Minotaur's point of view, the thread would not leave the maze; it therefore would wind, cross over, back up, and get tangled into knotted indirections. In the maze, caprice and invention thrive on their own meanderings. And one might guess that a man with the head of a bull would neither think nor speak straight; he must have a few loose threads hanging around.

I would like to think that "environmental" pressures of that kind led the Minotaur's hybrid words to bounce, skip, and jump along a playful tune of quasi-melodious cacophonies that would break up any narrative line. At its *Ur* point, therefore, the Daedalian locus housed an artform indeed akin to the mannerist passion for composite works of art. The voice of the gods came down from Olympus. Mankind's eccentricities instead were displaced amid Cretan youths who had been somersaulting over the bull's back since the earliest times.[5] Even Europa got to Crete by riding a bull.

When Jorge Luis Borges, a most labyrinthine mind of latter days, undertook his pursuit of knowledge in *The Library of Babel,* he "wandered in search of a book, perhaps the catalogues of catalogues. . . . The Library exists *ab aeterno.*" The Library is a universe of printed words all derived from "the twenty-five orthographical symbols." Borges also warned that "to speak is to fall into tautology." Nevertheless, the universe of knowledge could still operate as a world of words that would give free range to the testing potential of stylistic eccentricity. And the mannerist Minotaur was there to show strange ways whereby his bizarre rhetoric had reduced knowledge to a matter of alphabetical combinations aimed at arranging what had been said before.

If speaking was tautological amid Borgesian catalogues, mythic riddles threaded repetitive structures of sameness. To find Daedalus's whereabouts, so the story goes, the unforgiving Minos let it be known that a reward would go to whoever could solve his riddle, which J. Hillis Miller has thoughtfully paraphrased for us: "How to run a thread through all the chambers and intricate windings of a complex seashell? Daedalus pierces the center of the shell, ties a thread to an ant, puts the ant in the pierced whole, and wins the prize when the ant emerges at the mouth of the shell. Thread and labyrinth, thread intricately crinkled to and fro as the retracing of the labyrinth which defeats the labyrinth but makes another intricate web at the same time—pattern is here superimposed on pattern."[6] It goes without saying that Daedalus solved the riddle, even though it is not clear whether he collected the prize. What is clear is that the experience of the maze tends to linger on; it quantifies itself and finally makes a qualitative leap. The "maze" never left Daedalus, whose very mind became a meandering diagram of the archetypal maze-maker. Such a tautological "fix" would indeed be prone to yield mannerist intricacies.

IV

Having deserted Ariadne, Theseus went to the island of Delos to honor Apollo and Venus. He performed a dance whose intricate movements were nothing but a ritualized "repetition" of the labyrinth experience.

At the height of mannerist adulthood, rhetorical excess thrived on a tradition dating back to Aristotle and Horace, who set mimetic poetry apart from nonmimetic rhetoric. Whereas the *Poetics* centers on such narrative elements as plot, character, thought, and spectacle, the *Rhetoric* takes up invention, arrangement, and style; emphasis lies on exposition more than understanding and on the arrangement of images over the expression of ideas.[7] Cretan legends made an impact even on the mainland.

Richard Lanham's epigraph to this chapter takes up concerns with rhetoric as a parodic excess of that "rhetorical paideia whose aim was to create pleasure and approval."[8] To sketch the extravagant semblance of the Minotaur's "mannerist ethos," we might as well embody it in the *homo rhetoricus,* that is to say, the parodic and ebullient "other" of the moderate *homo seriosus.* The mannerist *homo rhetoricus* understood that perfection can be fulfilled only in the sphere of technique and playfulness. Accordingly, a perfect artist would be a perfect "routinier," a virtuoso, a master of the split-language of shape-shifters such as fools, clowns, and tricksters, whose metaphorical bent set up new configurations of phonemes, morphemes, and conundrums. The artist therefore would foster carnival reversals of official discourse.

With a vengeance, the *homo rhetoricus* lives for pleasure, game, and success. His poetry and prose are premeditated, and at arm's length from the mimetic discourse of narration, history, and ideology.[9] To borrow from Lanham, he assumes "a natural agility in changing orientations. He hits the street already streetwise. From birth, he was dwelt not in a single value-structure but in several." In his Arcimboldesque makeup, such a ludic face could indeed change directions and shift "mechanisms of identity,"[10] for he was the embodiment of mannerist displacements.

To be true to his mythic vocation, the Daedalian punster treated the morphology of form as a mechanism of bizarre productivity that gave full range to his mannerist treatment of language. In our own century, Wittgensteinian concerns with language have described tautology as a wheel running idle and contradiction as a wheel that got stuck (*Mathematical Notes* [1939]). To update my critical commentary in the shadow of the punster's eccentric mechanism, I would suggest that, like an engine running idle, mannerist language was active, but it did not shift meaning into gear. Bruno's cornucopian language sped up discourse, whereas his mannerist counterpart let it run idly, and so tampered with the gear box that it stalemated; it could rely on a fine tuning, but to no practical avail.

Having been nurtured in the "Lexicon Rhetoricae," the *homo rhetoricus* spelled the artful alphabet of figures of speech and appeared on the stage of life after the gods had created a harmonious cosmos.

V

Myth has it that Zeus himself was born on Crete. Perhaps myth's labyrinthine plan for bringing the Minotaur to life on that island stemmed from a "mannerist" impulse to test the metamorphic limits of Olympian eccentricity. One could bet that the gods already had put out their best efforts when they let the grotesque offspring of human excess come to life on a dance floor off the coast of Greece.

Myth tells us that the Minotaur was killed, the revolt of the giants was crushed, and the Tower of Babel was leveled to the ground. Even the gods perished. Somehow, however, the spirit of the maze-maker has survived. In fact, history tells us that Daedalian punsters have thrived since the dawn of time, and their labyrinthine rhetoric has engulfed us. Myth also tells us that the Minotaur was put away into a labyrinth. But Theseus would confess that too many of us have displaced its center within our own selves. The *homo artifex* defeated the gods. Yet his hybrid twin has had the best of him more than once.

As if moved by a tautological imperative, the Daedalian punster had to have the last laugh. To posterity's delight, his Arcimboldesque grin has kept on laughing at the doorstep of life's eccentricities.

Notes

Introduction

1. *European Literature and the Latin Middle Ages* (New York, 1968), 274. Also Rudolph and Margot Wittkower, *Born under Saturn: The Character and Conduct of Artists* (New York, 1969), 67–71, 78.

2. Michael Baxandall, *Painting and Experience in Fifteenth-Century Italy: A Primer in the Social History of Pictorial Style* (Oxford, 1972), 56; John Spencer, "Ut Rhetorica Pictura: A Study in Quattrocento Theory of Painting," *Journal of the Warburg and Courtauld Institutes* 20 (1957): 33; David Summers, "Contrapposto: Style and Meaning in Renaissance Art," *Art Bulletin* 59 (1977): 344–45.

3. John Shearman, *Mannerism* (Baltimore, 1967), 32–34, 44. On 136, the critic writes: "Contemporary standards do not give the right guidance to understanding a past age; indeed in most cases they are a positive hindrance. In decoding messages from the other side we get more meaningful results if we use their code rather than ours. To be realistic, we should acknowledge that we cannot entirely avoid the influence of the patterns of thought of our own time; yet it is possible to minimize the distortion they bring with them."

4. *The Light in Troy: Imitation and Discovery in Renaissance Poetry* (New Haven, 1982), 177.

5. *On Painting*, trans. J. Spencer (New Haven, 1973), 40. References are to this edition (*O.P.*), with page numbers indicated in the text.

6. In this connection, E. H. Gombrich writes that "Mannerism comes to its climax at the moment when the inherent ambiguities of the Renaissance idea of artistic progress become apparent—at the moment when, by common consent, Michelangelo has achieved 'perfection' by realizing the highest potentialities of his art"; in *Norm and Form: Studies in the Art of the Renaissance* (London, 1971), 9.

7. Ernesto Grassi, *Heidegger and the Question of Renaissance Humanism* (Binghamton, 1983), 15.

8. Baldassare Castiglione, *The Book of the Courtier*, trans. C. Singleton

(New York, 1959), 60; references are to this edition, with page numbers indicated in the text. Benedetto Varchi, *Opere,* vol. 2 (Trieste, 1858–59), 626. On the hyperbolic character of artistic epistolarity, see Paola Barocchi, *Studi vasariani* (Turin, 1984), 83–111.

9. As Thomas Greene comments, "the more the usable past narrows to one or two supreme figures, the more the past becomes, almost by definition, unattainable and unmatchable. . . . In the largely pro-Ciceronian treatises of the cinquecento, history remains an irrepressible embarrassment"; in *The Light in Troy,* 178. And Bernard Berenson would add that "nothing is so tyrannically exclusive and levelling as a firmly established reigning style! No faith is more intolerant"; in *Aesthetics and History* (New York, 1948), 161.

10. See Luciano Berti, *Il principe dello studiolo* (Florence, 1967), 148.

11. In his authoritative *Idea del Tempio della Pittura* (Rome, 1947). Translation by the author. The treatise was published between 1584 and 1590.

12. *The Letters of Matthew Arnold to Arthur Hugh Clough* (London, 1932), 97.

13. *Counter-Statement* (New York, 1931), 265. See also Curtius, *European Literature and the Latin Middle Ages,* 274.

14. *Il giardino dei sensi* (Vicenza, 1975); *Die Welt als Labyrinth* (Hamburg, 1957); *Mannerism,* 2 vols. (London, 1965); *L'Antirinascimento* (Milan, 1962).

15. In the wake of Benno Geiger's pioneering monograph, *I dipinti ghiribizzosi di Giuseppe Arcimboldi* (Florence, 1954), it has taken over twenty years of scholarship to produce book-length studies. See Achille Bonito-Oliva *Arcimboldo* (Parma, 1978); Francesco Porzio, *L'universo illusorio di Arcimboldi* (Milan, 1979). See also *Effetto Arcimboldo* (Milan, 1987), and the whole issue of *Art Dossier,* no. 11, with essays by Jurgis Baltrusaitis, Francesco Porzio, and Maurizio Calvesi. With regard to periodization, John Shearman clarifies that "no historical concept of Mannerism exists in the *Cinquecento,* but it is then that Maniera was most appreciated in works of art; in "Maniera as an Aesthetic Ideal," in *The Renaissance and Mannerism: Acts of the Twentieth International Congress of the History of Art,* vol. 2 (Princeton, 1963), 211. In a brief essay, Cesare Brandi gives a short paragraph to the central position that Arcimboldo held in relation to Mannerism; in *Segno e Immagine* (Palermo, 1986), 67.

16. *Trattati d'arte del Cinquencento,* vol. 3 (Bari, 1962), translations are mine. References are to this edition (*Trattati*), with volume and page number indicated in the text. Criticism of Comanini is limited. Julius Schlosser has minimized the significance of his work in *La letteratura artistica* (Florence, 1967), but Eugenio Battisti has paid greater attention to him in *Rinascimento a Barocco* (Turin, 1960), 210–12. Although limited to an outline, Paola Barocchi's comments still offer the best insight into the treatise. Carlo Ossola, *L'Autunno del Rinascimento* (Florence, 1971), 100–110, overrates the metamorphic character of the treatise in relation to Arcimboldo's canvases. A short monograph has been published by Anna Ferrari-Bravo, *Il Figino: Teoria della pittura di fine '500* (Rome, 1975).

17. Such a label included Arcimboldo, Bosch, Blake, and Henri Rousseau, who were to form the core of an unrealized exhibition (planned in 1948) at the

Galerie Maeght in Paris; reference in William Rubin, *Dada, Surrealism, and Their Heritage* (New York, 1968), 216.

18. In *Bracelli: Bizzarrie* (Paris, 1963), 5.

19. Francesco Porzio, *L'universo illusorio di Arcimboldo*, 5.

20. In *Manifestoes of Surrealism* (Ann Arbor, 1977), 16.

21. Wolfgang Kayser, *The Grotesque in Art and Literature* (Bloomington, 1963); Geoffrey Harpham, *On the Grotesque: Strategies of Contradiction in Art and Literature* (Princeton, 1982); Gustav René Hocke, *Manierismus in der Literatur* (Hamburg, 1959).

22. James Mirollo, *Mannerism and Renaissance Poetry: Concept, Mode, Inner Design* (New Haven, 1984), xi–xii.

23. *Manierismus in der Literatur*, 145.

24. See Margarita Levisi, "Las Figuras Compuestas en Arcimboldo y Quevedo," *Comparative Literature* 20 (1968): 217–35. Also her "Hieronymus Bosch y los *Sueños* de Francisco de Quevedo," *Filologia* 9 (1963): 163–200.

25. On the subject, see Rensselaer E. Lee, *Ut Pictura Poesis: The Humanist Theory of Painting* (New York, 1967); Leo Spitzer, *Classical and Christian Ideas of World Harmony* (Baltimore, 1963); Austin Caswell, "Giuseppe Arcimboldo: Mannerist in Music," *Journal of Aesthetics and Art Criticism* 49 (1969): 23–44. Jean Paris would suggest that "word and sight function together, like two instances of a single act; in *Painting and Linguistics* (Pittsburgh, 1975), 3, 25. On the related subject of *imprese*, see Andrea Gareffi, *Le voci dipinte: Figura e parola nel Manierismo italiano* (Rome, 1981), 13–19. Marcel Brion refers to Arcimboldo's invention of a *luth perspectif* based on the relation of color and sound, and of a *clavecin des couleurs* that anticipated the *clavecin oculaire* of Louis Castel, in *Art Fantastique* (Paris, 1961), 140–41. John Shearman, *Mannerism*, 32–34, generalizes as follows: "Too little appreciated is the extent to which the critical language of one of the arts in the sixteenth century was in fact common to all of them. This was only in part due to cross-fertilization; it was primarily due to the derivation in each case of critical techniques, frameworks and terms of reference from the enormous body of ancient criticism which was, as it happened, mainly literary and rhetorical, to a lesser extent musical, and scarcely at all concerned with the visual arts." Petrarchism brought to the emblematic tradition a penchant for antitheses and stereotyped phrases. Giulio Marzot insists that another proof "of the dissociation of Petrarchan forms from their spiritual substance during the sixteenth century is their usage in connection with the genre of *emblema* and *impresa*. . . . The combination of words and designs produced new relationships among the arts, which educated the eye to look at images polysemously"; in "Il tramite del Petrarchismo dal Rinascimento al Barocco," 140–41; also C. Meozzi, *Il petrarchismo europeo* (Pisa, 1934), xxi–xxiv; Georg Weise, *Manierismo e letteratura* (Florence, 1976), 54–55. Even the elements of landscape—plants, flowers, sky—could turn into mental forms. Cesare Ripa personified the Year as an "aged and bearded man . . . draped with flowers (for spring), ears of corn (for summer), and grapes (for autumn); in *Iconologia*, as translated by E. Maser as *Baroque and Rococo Pictorial Imagery* (New York, 1971), 17. This description is strikingly similar to Comanini's remarks on a lost picture of the same subject painting by Arcimboldo. *Imprese* heightened the contiguity of pictures

and poems (Caburacci, Ammirato) amid a literary milieu that was indeed familiar to Arcimboldo; see Enrico Castelli, "Umanesimo e simbolismo involontario," in *Umanesimo e Simbolismo: Atti del VI Congresso Internazionale di Studi Umanistici* (Padua, 1958), 21. In conjunction with structural indirections, Petrarchism also affected the poetic tradition of the blazon, which listed the various parts of a woman's body through a surfacelike catalogue of physical attributes. The convention quickly became a cliché that spawned the mutant of counter-blazons. In that parodic framework, experimentations with the sonnet form (Lomazzo) were akin to Arcimboldo's stylistic conceits; on the subject, see Edoardo Taddeo, "I grilli poetici di un pittore: Le *Rime* di G.P. Lomazzo," 152–53. J. A. Cuddon, *A Dictionary of Literary Terms* (New York, 1976), 85–86. In fact, *The Cook* shared with less than polite *poèmes gourmands* a mock-heroic mode whereby "armored" cookware figures parodied chivalric images; See D. B. Wilson, *Descriptive Poetry in France from Blason to Baroque* (New York, 1967), 222–23. At closer distance, one finds Colonna's *Hypnerotomachia Poliphili,* the first *libro illustrato* that mixed mathematics, hieroglyphs, pictorial illustrations, and architectural descriptions. Colonna, Alciati, and Ripa provided dictionaries for artists who looked on poetry as a "*peinture parlante*"; see Marcel Raymond, "La Pléiade et le Maniérisme," in *Lumières de la Pléiade: Neuvième Stage International d'Etudes Humanistes. Tours 1965* (Paris, 1966), 395. The emphasis on the visual was overwhelming.

26. *The Lion and the Honeycomb: Essays in Solicitude and Critique* (New York, 1955), 182–83.

27. This methodological position confirms—verbatim—what I have written in my *The Cornucopian Mind and the Baroque Unity of the Arts* (University Park, Pa., 1990), 8–9.

Chapter 1

1. *On Longing: Narratives of the Miniature, the Gigantic, the Souvenir, the Collection* (Baltimore, 1984), ix.

2. Translations are from *The Lives of the Artists,* ed. and trans. Julia Conaway Bondanella and Peter Bondanella (Oxford, 1991). I acknowledge their kindness in letting me use their forthcoming volume, which is indeed much needed in Vasari studies and mannerist scholarship.

3. *Il gusto dei primitivi* (Turin, 1972), 86. This text focuses on the relation between perfection and praxis.

4. See Madeleine Frederic, "Le tautologie dans le langage naturel," *Travaux de linguistique et de littérature* 19 (1981): 313–14.

5. *Figures,* vol. 1 (Paris, 1966), 28. Also his "La rhétorique restreinte," *Communications* 16 (1970): 168; Catherine Kerbrat-Orecchioni, *La connotation* (Lyon, 1977), 140–41; C. Perelman and L. Olbrechts Tyteca, *Traité de l'argumentation: La Nouvelle rhétorique* (Brussels, 1970), 292. Josette Rey-Debove, "Le sens de la tautologie," *Le Français Moderne* 46 (1978): 328, writes: "Il n'y a jamais tautologie. . . . Tout truisme, toute relation d'identité

attestent, en un certain sens, un progrès, un mouvement, au moins dans l'énonciation," For an extensive and analytical study of repetition, see Madeleine Frederic, *La répétition: Etude linguistique et rhétorique* (Tübingen, 1985), especially the pages on pleonasm and tautology (68–70, 109–24).

6. See Edoardo Saccone, "Grazia, Sprezzatura, and Affettazione in Castiglione's *Book of the Courtier,*" *Glyph* 5 (1979): 44–46.

7. "Michelangelo on Effort and Rapidity in Art," *Journal of the Warburg and Courtauld Institutes* 17 (1954): 309. Richard A. Lanham, *The Motives of Eloquence: Literary Rhetoric in the Renaissance* (New Haven, 1976), 152, writes that *sprezzatura* "declares, brags about, successful enselfment, a permanent incorporation in, addition to, the self." In *Analyzing Prose* (New York, 1983), 247, Lanham adds that "this sleazy compromise has lasted as a stylistic bromide ever since." In turn, *sprezzatura* "seems hopelessly self-contradictory, an artistic kind of artlessness, a carefully studied but unself-conscious presentation of self, a contrived naturalness." And again, Lanham points out that "*sprezzatura* was a new word for a new conception of identity, that paradoxically natural unnaturalness, sense of effortless effort, of instinctive artifice"; in *Literacy and the Survival of Humanism* (New Haven, 1983), 36. A similar problem affects *préciosité,* as Odette de Mourgues writes: "Whereas, in the case of the baroque, critics have looked for a concise formula—such as the baroque as the art of the Counter-Reformation—in the case of the précieux they have, as a rule, circled round their object, noting characteristics, making one daring step forward in asserting, for instance, that préciosité should not be assimilated to *la galanterie*. . . . we are given not one definition but a string of characteristics"; in *Metaphysical, Baroque and Précieux Poetry* (Oxford, 1953), 105. On associative and lexical fields, see Stephen Ullmann, *Language and Style* (Oxford, 1964), 222.

8. See Attila Fay, "Vico as Philosopher of *Metabasis,*" in *Giambattista Vico's Science of Humanity,* ed. G. Tagliacozzo and D. P. Verene (Baltimore, 1976), 87–109.

9. *Letters from Petrarch,* trans. M. Bishop (Bloomington, 1966), 199.

10. *The Family in Renaissance Florence,* trans. R. Watkins (Columbia, Mo., 1969), 250. The title translates as *I libri della famiglia* (1437–41).

11. As Schiller wrote about Beauty, "Its whole magic resides in its mystery, and in disclosing the essential amalgam of its elements we find we have dissolved its very Being" (*On the Aesthetic Education of Man,* first letter, 5).

12. See Thomas Greene, "Petrarch and the Humanist Hermeneutic," in *Italian Literature: Roots and Branches,* ed. G. Rimanelli and K. J. Atchity (New Haven, 1976), 210–12.

13. I follow here the main argument of my *Adam "New Born and Perfect": The Renaissance Promise of Eternity* (Bloomington, 1987). Also John Pope-Hennessy, *Italian High Renaissance and Baroque Sculpture* (London, 1963), 61; E. H. Gombrich, "A Classical Topos in the Introduction to Alberti's *Della Pittura,*" *Journal of the Warburg and Courtauld Institutes* 20 (1957): 173; and Mary D. Garrard, "The Liberal Arts and Michelangelo's First Project for the Tomb of Julius II (with a Coda on Raphael's 'School of Athens')," *Viator* 15 (1984): 335–76. On relations between praise and epistolarity, see Paola Barocchi, *Studi vasariani* (Turin, 1984), 84–87.

14. *European Literature and the Latin Middle Ages,* 163–64. On the man-

nerist character of such leanings, see Marcel Raymond, *La poésie française et le Maniérisme, 1546–1610* (Geneva, 1971), 28–99; Hugo Friedrich, *Epochen der Italianischen Lyrik* (Munich, 1964), 546.

15. See Eugenio Battisti's *L'antirinascimento* (Milan, 1962), 163; Giulio Ferroni and Amedeo Quondam, *La "locuzione artificiosa": Teoria ed esperienza della lirica a Napoli nell'età del manierismo* (Rome, 1973), 82.

16. Giovanni Nencioni, *Tra grammatica e retorica* (Turin, 1983), 87.

17. Postscript to *Appreciations* (London, 1924), 258–59. This thesis is repeated in *Greek Studies* (London, 1911) and in *Plato and Platonism* (London, 1912). Also Harold Bloom's Introduction to *Selected Writings of Walter Pater* (New York, 1974), especially xxx.

18. *Aristotle's Poetics: The Argument* (Cambridge, 1963), 495.

19. *Language in Thought and Action* (New York, 1964), 219–20.

20. With an eye to the fundamental work of the Liège Group, tropes and figures constitute "*une modification du niveau de redondance calculable du code, perçue grâce à une impertinence distributionelle.*" The result is not a progressively linear but a visually simultaneous ("*tabulaire*") reading. See *Rhétorique de la poésie,* ed. J. Dubois, F. Edeline, J. M. Klinkenberg, and P. Minguet (Brussels, 1977), 46–47.

21. See Martin Foss, *The Idea of Perfection* (Princeton, 1946), 58–59.

22. *Aesthetics* (New York, 1964), 183–85. John Shearman writes: "Mannerism should, by tradition, speak a silver-tongued language of articulate, if unnatural, beauty, not one of incoherence, menace and despair; it is, in a phrase, the stylish style"; in *Mannerism,* 19.

23. Luigi Grassi, *Teorici e storia della critica d'arte,* vol. 1 (Rome, 1970), 214.

24. In Quondam and Ferroni, *La "locuzione artificiosa,"* 106. We might agree with the two critics that the mannerists viewed the realities of mind and nature through a tautological code that was at once a "system of repetition" and an "experience of differences"; in ibid., 223–24. Also Amedeo Quondam, *Petrarchismo mediato* (Rome, 1974), 220–22.

25. *A Map of Misreading* (New York, 1975), 74, 102, 93.

26. Quondam and Ferroni, *La "locuzione artificiosa,"* 225; André Chastel, "Le Fragmentaire, l'Hybride, et l'Inachevé," in J. A. Schmoll Eisenwerth, *Das Unvollendete als Kunstlerische Form: Ein Symposion* (Bern, 1959), 90–91; Lanham, *The Motives of Eloquence,* 29.

27. John Shearman, *Mannerism* (Baltimore, 1967), 171.

Chapter 2

1. This stylistic trait is typically mannerist for Panofsky, in *Idea: A Concept in Art Theory* (New York, 1968), 74. Likewise, Arnold Hauser found in Parmigianino's "overloading of the foreground a mannerist trait," in *Mannerism,* 1:204. Also John Shearman, "Maniera as an Aesthetic Ideal," in *The*

Renaissance and Mannerism: Acts of the Twentieth International Congress of the History of Art, vol. 2 (Princeton, 1963), 182.

2. See Panofsky, *Idea: A Concept in Art Theory,* 90–92; Gustav René Hocke, *Manierismus in der Literatur* (Hamburg, 1959), 13–14; Mario Praz's chapter on *sculture bizzarre,* in *Il giardino dei sensi,* 62–70.

3. *Arcimboldo,* 62.

4. See R. E. Wolf and R. Millen, *Renaissance and Mannerist Art* (New York, 1968), 81. Murray Roston, *Renaissance Perspectives in Literature and the Visual Arts* (Princeton, 1987), 309.

5. *Die Welt als Labyrinth* (Hamburg, 1957), 78. On Leonardo's anamorphoses, see *Codex Atlanticus,* fol. 35v., 1485, Biblioteca Ambrosiana, Milan. Fred Leeman, *Hidden Images. Games of Perception. Anamorphic Art. Illusion. From the Renaissance to the Present* (New York, 1976), 10–11. Also Carlo Pedretti, "Un soggetto anamorfico, in *Studi vinciani* (Geneva, 1957), 68–76; Jurgis Baltrusaitis, *Anamorphic Art* (New York, 1977); Fabrizio Clerici, "The Grand Illusion: Some Considerations of Perspective, Illusionism, and Trompe l'oeil," *Art News Annual* 23 (1954): 109, 120; J. C. Margolin, "Aspects du Surréalisme au xvi-siècle: Fonction allegorique et vision anamorphotique," in *Bibliothèque d'Humanisme et Renaissance* 39 (1977): 507–11.

6. See Arthur Schopenhauer, *The World as Will and Representation,* vol. 2, trans. E. F. J. Payne (New York, 1966), 335–36; Ezio Raimondi's introduction to Tesauro in his edition of *Trattatisti e narratori del Seicento* (Milan, 1960), 20; Giacomo Devoto, *Profilo di storia linguistica italiana* (Florence, 1964), 90; Mario Praz, *Il giardino dei sensi* (Vicenza, 1975), 36; Carlo Ossola, "Rassegna di testi e studi del manierismo e Barocco," *Lettere italiane* 27 (1975): 453–55.

7. See Angus Fletcher, *Allegory: The Theory of a Symbolic Mode* (Ithaca, 1970), 230. W. M. Urban, *Language and Reality* (London, 1939), 112; Stephen Ullman, *Language and Style,* 75–77.

8. *Arcimboldo,* 30.

9. *Peculiar Language: Literature as Difference from the Renaissance to James Joyce* (Ithaca, N.Y., 1988), 108–9.

10. See Albert Henry, *Métonymie et Métaphore* (Paris, 1971), 77–78; S. J. Freedberg, "Observations on the Painting of Maniera," *Art Bulletin* 47 (1965): 189; Susan Stewart, *On Longing: Narratives of the Miniature, the Gigantic, the Souvenir, the Collection* (Baltimore, 1984), 74.

11. *Les structures anthropologiques de l'imaginaire* (Poitiers, 1969), 490. On linguistic techniques, see Tzvetan Todorov, "Synecdoches," *Communications* 16 (1970): 31.

12. *Early Renaissance* (Baltimore, 1967), 80.

13. As translated in David Summers, *Michelangelo and the Language of Art* (Princeton, 1981), 210–11; see his comments, 103, 109–10, 128–29.

14. *Leonardo da Vinci: The Marvelous Works of Nature and Man* (London, 1981), 160.

15. Machines carried symbolic connotations during the Middle Ages but later claimed autonomy from philosophy and religion. The *automi* thus colonized provinces where human ingenuity mastered water (fountains), fire (*giochi pirotecnici* and the gigantic *incendi* at Castel Sant'Angelo and Piazza

Navona in Rome), and fable. See Eugenio Battisti, *L'Antirinascimento* (Milan, 1962), 230–36. Also Jurgis Baltrusaitis, *Le Miroir* (Paris, 1978).

16. Robert Harbison, *Eccentric Spaces* (New York, 1977), 42. Francesco I sponsored a new *mecenatismo scientifico* that benefited artists like Buontalenti and Giambologna. In Villa Demidoff at Pratolino, the *Dux Mechanicus* enjoyed *teatri d'automi* (located in six grottoes), which brought to a head a sustained curiosity about geometric forms. Earlier, Paolo Uccello had reduced soldiers to puppetlike shapes (the San Romano battle pieces) enacting a "rusty dream of invulnerability" on stages where clatter made noise but did no harm.

17. See Mary Ann Caws, *The Eye in the Text: Essays on Perception, Mannerist to Modern* (Princeton, 1981), 135–37.

18. See James Mirollo, *Mannerism and Renaissance Poetry: Concept, Mode, Inner Design,* 99–101.

19. See Paul Valéry, *Degas, Manet, Morisot* (New York, 1960), 205; Robert Harbison, *Eccentric Spaces,* 140–47.

20. De Chirico's museum canvases call to mind the mannerist (Francesco I) tradition of the *giardino antiquario,* in which the gathering of exotic flora complemented, so to speak, Giambologna's array of rare beasts in the grotto of Villa Medici (1540). Re-creations of the worlds of history and nature in a single place were just as artificial as surrealist treatments of the same subject.

21. See Bruno Migliorini, *Lingua e cultura* (Rome, 1948), 20; Battisti, *L'antirinascimento,* 129; Paola Barocchi, in *Trattati,* 3:398; Francine Claire Legrand and Félix Sluys, *Arcimboldo et les Arcimboldesques* (Aaltar, 1955), 13; S. J. Freedberg, "Observations on the Painting of Maniera," 189; Saussure, *Cours de linguistique général* (Paris, 1955).

22. "Théorie de la figure," *Communications* 16 (1970): 25. See Jurgis Baltrusaitis, *Anamorphic Art,* 81; Gustav René Hocke, *Die Welt als Labyrinth* (Hamburg, 1957), 96.

23. *Giorgio Vasari: Scrittore* (Pisa, 1905), 203. See also Achille Bonito-Oliva, *L'ideologia del traditore: Arte, Maniera, Manierismo* (Milan, 1981), 200.

24. In *Scritti scelti di Pietro Aretino e Anton Francesco Doni* (Turin, 1962), 428.

25. Terence Cave, *The Cornucopian Text: Problems of Writing in the French Renaissance* (Oxford, 1979), xviii.

26. *Discorsi dell'arte poetica e del poema eroico* (Bari, 1959), 209. Translation mine.

27. Elusive forms of that sort could be conceived only in a self-fulfilling state of isolation—"*favellare spesso da se medesimo*"—midway between wake and sleep ("*sonneferare*"); in Gelli's *Capricci del bottaio* (1548), in *Opere di Giovan Battista Gelli* (Turin, 1968), 148. Translation by author. Doni also associated the word *ghiribizzoso* with an extravagant and fantastic mind—*cervel balzano, fantastico, ghiribizzoso*—in *Scritti scelti di Pietro Aretino e di Anton Francesco Doni,* 427.

28. See Carlo Ossola, *L'Autunno del Rinascimento* (Florence, 1971), 173–74; Geoffrey Harpham, *On the Grotesque: Strategies of Contradiction in Art and Literature* (Princeton, 1982), 8.

29. See Anthony Blunt, *Artistic Theory in Italy 1450–1600* (London, 1968), 91.

30. See Bernard Weinberg's *A History of Literary Criticism in the Italian Renaissance* (Chicago, 1961), 2:774; Giovanni Nencioni, *Tra grammatica e retorica* (Turin, 1983), 78–79. For Mannerism in Prague under Rudolph II, see R. J. W. Evans, *Rudolph II and His World* (Oxford, 1973), especially 162–95, 243–74.

31. *A Grammar of Motives* (Berkeley, 1974), 504.

32. Grahame Castor, *Pléiade Poetics: A Study in Sixteenth-Century Thought and Terminology* (Cambridge, 1964), 126–29.

33. On the subject of perspective as a symbolic form, see Erwin Panofsky's fundamental essay, "Die Perspektive also 'symbolische Form,' " *Vorträge der Bibliothek Warburg* 4 (1924–25): 258–330; also Giulio Carlo Argan, "Origins of Perspective Theory in the Fifteenth Century," *Journal of the Warburg and Courtauld Institutes* 9 (1946): 100. See also Harald Weinrich, "Semantik der Kuhnen Metapher," in *Deutsche Vierteljahrsschrift für Literaturwissenschaft und Geistesgeschichte,* 37 n. 3, 335; Gilbert Ryle, *The Concept of Mind* (London, 1949), 16.

34. *S/Z* (New York, 1974), 9.

35. "On Truth and Falsehood in Their Extra-Moral Sense," in *The Complete Works of Nietzsche,* vol. 2, *Early Greek Philosophy,* ed. O. Levy (London, 1911), 180.

36. "Il Minturo over de la bellezza," in Ettore Mazzali's edition of Tasso's *Dialoghi,* in *Opere* (Naples, 1969), 2: 315, 321, 328. See Mazzali's comments, 355; Giuliano Briganti, *Italian Mannerism* (Leipzig, 1962), 13; Freedberg, "Observations on the Painting of Maniera," 191.

37. See Adalgisa Lugli, *Naturalia et Mirabilia* (Milan, 1983).

38. *Meaning in the Visual Arts* (New York, 1955), 136.

39. See E. R. Curtius, *European Literature and the Latin Middle Ages* (New York, 1963), 274, 282; André Pieyre de Mandiargue, *Arcimboldo the Marvelous* (New York, 1977), 88.

Chapter 3

1. *Marvels and Commonplaces: Renaissance Literary Criticism* (New York, 1968), vii.

2. See Grahame Castor, *Pleiade Poetics: A Study in Sixteenth-Century Thought and Terminology* (Cambridge, 1964), 116–17.

3. *Il cannocchiale aristotelico,* in *Trattatisti e narratori del Seicento,* ed. Ezio Raimondi (Milan, 1960), 91. Also Claude-Gilbert Dubois, *Le Maniérisme* (Paris, 1979), 26–27; Gustav René Hocke, *Die Welt als Labyrinth* (Hamburg, 1957), 48–49.

4. See Castor, *Pleiade Poetics,* 116–17.

5. See Johan Huizinga, *Homo Ludens: A Study of the Play-Element in Culture* (Boston, 1962), 35–36, 46, 119; Emile Benveniste, "Le jeu comme structure," *Deucalion* 2 (1947): 163–65.

6. *Early Renaissance,* 79; Huizinga, *Homo Ludens,* 8.

7. See Clayton Koelb, *Inventions of Reading: Rhetoric and the Literary Imagination* (Ithaca, N.Y., 1988), 46.

8. On Bomarzo, see *Bomarzo,* in *Quaderni dell'Istituto di Storia dell'Architettura,* 7–9, monograph no. 1955; A. Bruschi, "Il Problema storico di Bomarzo," *Palladio* 13 (1963): 85–114; J. Theurillat, *Les mystères de Bomarzo* (Geneva, 1973); Horst Bredekamp, *Vicino Orsini und der Heilige Wald von Bomarzo,* 2 vols. (Worms, 1985). Now translated into Italian, *Vicino Orsini e il Bosco Sacro di Bomarzo. Un Principe Artista ed Anarchico* (Rome, 1989).

9. *Bomarzo,* trans. Gregory Rabassa (New York, 1969), 484.

10. Giovanni de Bardi (*Discorso sopra il gioco del calcio fiorentino*) spoofed Platonic and Aristotelian categories on the subject of soccer; its final goal is scoring, the player is the material cause, and the rich nobleman picking up the tab is its efficient counterpart. On the same subject, Pontormo's *Study of a Nude Playing Calcio* made fun of Michelangelo. Pontormo's *Study of the Three Graces* also took on Botticelli and Raphael. See Paul Barolsky's fundamental study, *Infinite Jest: Wit and Humor in Italian Renaissance Art* (Columbia, Mo., 1978).

11. Julius Held, "Flora, Goddess and Courtesan," in *Essays in Honor of Erwin Panofsky,* ed. Millard Meiss (New York, 1961), 206; Anthony Blunt, *Artistic Theory in Italy 1450–1600* (London, 1968), 89.

12. In John Shearman, *Mannerism,* 156. For the critic, "this is not necessarily a clue to understanding Piero's paintings, but it is revealing for the taste of the society in which it was written."

13. It is not clear at all which, among the surviving canvases, is Arcimboldo's. Their plurality is problematic, and this is not the place to raise matters of attribution. All versions, however, deal with a figure made of flowers. To that extent they are equally relevant within the thematic context of this study. To be cautious, Figures 7 and 18 present two versions that seem to "cover" the range between authentic Arcimboldo and the Arcimboldesque.

14. Geoffrey Harpham, *On the Grotesque: Strategies of Contradictions in Art and Literature* (Princeton, 1962), 6; Northrop Frye, *Anatomy of Criticism* (New York, 1969), 275. Also Michael B. Kline, *Rabelais and the Age of Printing* (Geneva, 1963), 40; François Rigolot, "Poétiques Marginales au xvi et au xvii siècles," *Revue de littérature comparée* 51 (1977): 226; Forrest G. Robinson, *The Shape of Things Known: Sidney's Apology in Its Philosophical Tradition* (Cambridge, Mass., 1972), 88, 96; Walter J. Ong, *Ramus, Method, and the Decay of Dialogue* (Cambridge, 1958). For a recent study on the subject, see Willard Bohn, *The Aesthetics of Visual Poetry 1914–1928* (Cambridge, 1986), especially 3–5.

15. Within the tradition of *fratrasies*-Burchiello-Doni-Lomazzo, the genre well served the "*poeta pittor di grottesche.* Reference in Edoardo Taddeo, "I grilli poetici di un pittore: Le *Rime* di G.P. Lomazzo," 177; P. Zumthor, "Jonglerie et langage," *Poétique* 11 (1972): 333; Marco Ariani, "Il 'puro artifizio.' Scrittura tropica e dissoluzione melica nella Canace di Sperone Speroni," *Il contrasto* 3 (1977): 94.

16. *Dialogo della Retorica,* in *Trattati del Cinquecento,* vol. 1, ed. Mario Pozzi (Milan, 1978), 642–43, Translation mine. See Gérard Genette, *Figures,* vol. 1, 250; Carlo Ossola, *Autunno del Rinascimento,* 87.

17. *The Incredulous Reader: Literature and the Function of Disbelief* (Ithaca, 1984), 37, 41, 57, 228–30.

18. *The Treatise on Painting*, vol. 1, ed. A. P. McMahon (Princeton, 1956), 277.

19. See his Introduction to *Two Tales of the Occult* (New York, 1970), x. On Ovid and Vertumnus, see Leonard Barkan, *The Gods Made Flesh: Metamorphosis and the Pursuit of Paganism* (New York, 1986), 82. On the antiportrait in a surrealist context, see Renée Riese Hubert, "L'antiportrait surréaliste," in *Théorie. Tableau. Texte,* ed. M. A. Caws (Paris, 1978), 6.

20. The sonnet is included in Amedeo Quondam and Giulio Ferroni, *La "locuzione artificiosa": Teoria ed esperienza della lirica a Napoli nell'età del manierismo* (Rome, 1973), 374.

21. *The Poetics of Space* (New York, 1964), 149; Lionel Abel, *Metatheater: A New View of Dramatic Form* (New York, 1963), 72.

22. *Literature and Liminality: Festive Readings in the Hispanic Tradition* (Durham, 1986), xiii; Victor Turner, *Dramas, Fields, and Metaphors: Symbolic Action in Human Society* (Ithaca, N.Y., 1974).

23. Pérez Firmat, *Literature and Liminality: Festive Readings in the Hispanic Tradition* (Durham, N.C., 1986), xvii; Mikhail Bakhtin, *Rabelais and His World* (Cambridge, Mass., 1968); Natalie Zemon Davis, *Society and Culture in Early Modern France* (Stanford, 1975), 100.

24. "Le due anime nelle ville della Tuscia," in *Il giardino d'Europa: Pratolino come modello nella cultura europea* (Milan, 1986), 70.

Chapter 4

1. *Mannerism and Anti-Mannerism in Italian Painting* (New York, 1969), 48.

2. See Giulio Ferroni and Amedeo Quondam, *La "locuzione artificiosa": Teoria della lirica a Napoli nell'età del manierismo* (Rome, 1973), 82.

3. See John Shearman, "Maniera as an Aesthetic Ideal," 202; Craig Hugh Smyth, "Mannerism and Maniera," 179; and Georg Weise, "La doppia origine del concetto di Manierismo," in *Studi vasariani* (Florence, 1952), 185.

4. *The Heroic Frenzies,* trans. Paul Memmo (Chapel Hill, 1964), 83. I have set Bruno's view within a baroque contextuality in *The Cornucopian Mind and the Baroque Unity of the Arts,* especially chapter 4.

5. S. J. Freedberg, *Painting in Italy, 1500 to 1600,* 417; Arnold Hauser, *Mannerism,* vol. 1, 283. Recently James Mirollo has written that literary mannerism sought in phenomena such as Petrarchism a "parodic juxtaposition to, even a parasitic dependence upon, a thematic and stylistic model"; in *Mannerism and Renaissance Poetry: Concept, Mode, Inner Design* (New Haven, 1984), 69.

6. "Mannerism and Maniera," 175.

7. See Walter Friedlaender, "The Anticlassical Style," in *Mannerism and Anti-Mannerism in Italian Painting.*

8. *The Life and Art of Albrecht Dürer* (Princeton, 1955), 274; *Idea: A Concept in Art Theory* (New York, 1968), 72.

9. Helmut Hatzfeld, "Camoes' manieristische und Tassos barocke Gestaltung des Nymphenmotivs," *Aufsätze zur portugiesischen Kulturgeschichte* 3 (1962–63): 106; Georg Weise, *Manierismo e letteratura* (Florence, 1976), 57.

10. *The Expulsion of the Triumphant Beast*, trans. Arthur Imerti (New Brunswick, 1964), 78.

11. See "The Breaking of the Circle: Giordano Bruno and the Poetics of Immeasurable Abundance," in my *The Cornucopian Mind and the Baroque Unity of the Arts*. Parenthetically, scholarship on Ovid's *Metamorphoses* tends to emphasize baroque rather than mannerist analogues. On the subject, see Ettore Paratore, "L'influenza della letteratura latina da Ovidio ad Apuleio nell'età del Manierismo e del Barocco," in *Manierismo. Barocco. Rococo: Concetti e Termini* (Rome, 1962), 239–301; R. Crahay, "La vision poétique d'Ovide et l'esthétique baroque," in *Atti del Convegno Internazionale Ovidiano*, vol. 1 (Rome, 1959), 91–110. Within this context, Bakhtin's concept of grotesque realism would be closer to the baroque: "The grotesque image reflects a phenomenon in transformation, an as yet unfinished metamorphosis, of death and birth, growth and becoming. The relation to time is one determining trait of the grotesque image"; *Rabelais and His World*, trans. Helene Iswolsky (Cambridge, Mass., 1968), 24.

12. John Shearman, *Mannerism* (Baltimore, 1967), 149. On rhetorical grounds, Amedeo Quondam draws a line between the mannerist preference for repetition, accumulation, enumeration, plurality, anaphora, and correlation vis-à-vis the baroque reliance on metaphor and metonymy. This distinction is valid in terms of emphasis, but we can think of instances (Tasso, Bruno, Marino, Tesauro, Borromini) that could prove the case either way; in *La parola nel labirinto: Società e scrittura del Manierismo a Napoli* (Bari, 1975), 6–7.

13. See Ulrich Weisstein, "Collage, Montage, and Related Terms: Their Literary and Figurative Use in and Application to Techniques and Forms in Various Arts," *Comparative Literature Studies* 15 (1978): 126; William C. Seitz, *The Art of Assemblage* (New York, 1961), 83; William Rubin, "De Chirico and Modernism," in *De Chirico* (New York, c. 1982), 63–64; J. H. Matthews, *Languages of Surrealism* (Columbia, Mo., 1986), 140, 146; Walter J. Ong, *Ramus: Method and the Decay of Dialogue* (Cambridge, Mass., 1958), 314–18.

14. Mario Praz, *Il giardino dei sensi* (Vicenza, 1975), 33. Also Bartlett Giamatti, "Proteus Unbound: Some Versions of the Sea God in the Renaissance," in *The Disciplines of Criticism*, ed. P. Demetz, T. Greene, and L. Nelson (New Haven, 1968), 450–51. On the centrality of metamorphosis in baroque art, see Jean Rousset, *La littérature de l'âge baroque en France: Circe et le paon* (Paris, 1968).

15. In "A Pamphlet on Imitation," in Izora Scott's *The Imitation of Cicero* (New York, 1910), 12.

16. Marcel Raymond draws similar conclusions with regard to mannerist poetry in *Etre et Dire: Etudes* (Neuchâtel, 1970), 134.

17. See Bruno Maier's comments in his edition of Tasso's *Opere,* vol. 1 (Milan, 1963), 206.

18. *Dialoghi,* vol. 2, ed. Ettore Mazzali (Turin, 1976), 326. Translation by author.

19. Likewise, the mythic stories in Giulio Romano's *Sala delle Metamorfosi* (Palazzo del Tè, Mantua) have little to do with the theme. Only nymphs and satyrs point to Ovidian references that remain strictly literary. See Frederick Hartt, *Giulio Romano,* vol. 1 (New Haven, 1958), 111–12.

20. *The Heroic Frenzies,* 63.

21. Labyrinths can be above ground, underground (grottoes, catacombs), and on ceilings (San Carlo alle Quattro Fontane in Rome). The directionless design on the ceiling of the Sala del Labirinto in the Palazzo Ducale at Mantua fully complements Vincenzo IV Gonzaga's equivocal motto, "*Forse che si, forse che no*" (maybe yes, maybe no). Above ground, the term maze in Anglo-Saxon languages derives from "maes," which means lawn; it also stands as root of "amazement," which is the effect that labyrinths and mazelike gardens produce. In German, *Irragarten* and *Garten* refer to garden-labyrinths as heirs to the classical *hortus conclusus.* Francesco Colonna reconstructed one of them in his *Hypnerotomachia Poliphili* (1499), where the dream of Poliphilo entails his coming out of an "*obscura Silva*" similar to Theseus's task of "*uscir del discolo labyrintho.*" Colonna's work is included in the volume on Iacopo Sannazaro's *Opere,* ed. Enrico Carrara (Turin, 1952), 276. On the sixteenth-century symbolism of the labyrinth, see Guy de Tervarent, *Attributs et Symboles dans l'art profane 1450–1600,* vol. 2 (Geneva, 1959), 39, and supplement (Geneva, 1964), 435. Also Paolo Santarcangelo, *Il libro dei labirinti* (Florence, 1967), 48–50, 72–73.

22. *Semiotics and the Philosophy of Language* (Bloomington, 1984), 81.

23. Robert Harbison, *Eccentric Spaces* (New York, 1977), 8–19.

24. *A Meaning to the Maze* (London, 1974), 4–5.

25. *The Family in Renaissance Florence,* trans. R. Watkins (Columbia, Mo., 1969), 206.

26. In *Surrealists on Art,* ed. Lucy R. Lippard (Englewood Cliffs, N.J., 1970), 56.

27. *Fantastic Art. Dada. Surrealism* (New York, 1936), 7. See illustrations of the two pictures in this volume.

28. Quoted in Massimo Carrà, *Metaphysical Art* (New York, 1971), 20.

29. "Observations on the Painting of the Maniera," *Art Bulletin* 47 (1965): 189–90.

30. *Ceci n'est pas une pipe* (Montpellier, 1973), 37. Filiberto Menna, "La trahison des images," in his edition of *Studi sul Surrealismo* (Rome, 1977), 322, speaks of "*scollamento*" (ungluing) of images.

31. René Magritte, *Tutti gli scritti,* ed. André Blavier (Milan, 1979), 465–66.

32. *Il giardino dei sensi,* 35.

33. See *Metaphysical Art,* 89.

34. "Impressionismo," in *Valori plastici,* vol. 1 (1919), 26, as translated in J. T. Solby, *Giorgio de Chirico* (New York, 1966), 41–42.

35. De Chirico, in *Metaphysical Art,* 89. Arnold Hauser, *Mannerism,* vol. 1, 371, refers to a common "dualism of fundamental outlook."

36. *The Philosophy of Surrealism* (Ann Arbor, 1965), 124.

37. Quotation and criticism from H. W. Janson, "The Image Made by chance in Renaissance Thought," in *Essays in Honor of Erwin Panofsky,* vol. 1, ed. Millard Meiss (New York, 1961), 254. See also E. H. Gombrich, *Art and Illusion* (Princeton, 1972), 181–202, 105–6.

38. Leonardo, *The Notebooks of Leonardo da Vinci,* vol. 1, ed. J. P. Richter (New York, 1970), 254; DaCosta Kaufmann, "Le allegorie e i loro significati," in *Effetto Arcimboldo* (Milan, 1987), 93. Even Anton Francesco Doni (*Il disegno,* 1549) linked chance images to the fantastic and the grotesque. See Luigi Grassi, *Teorici e storia della critica d'arte* (Rome, 1970), 168–69; Patrik Reutersward, "The Face in the Rock," *Art News Annual* 36 (1970): 99–110; Max Ernst, *Beyond Painting and Other Writings* (New York, 1948).

39. Leonardo da Vinci, *The Notebooks of Leonardo da Vinci,* vol. 1, ed. E. MacCurdy (New York, 1939), 1106. See Francesco Gandolfo, *Il "Dolce Tempo." Mistica, Ermetismo e Sogno nel Cinquecento* (Rome, 1978), 50, 218–19, 171–73, 279–81. With an eye to iconography, Annibal Caro centered on contemplative life in his program for the Stanza dei Sogni of Palazzo Farnese at Caprarola. Closer to our argument are Primaticcio's drawings for the *Porte Dorée* at Fontainebleau (1541–44?). In *Iride alla Casa del Sonno,* the realm of sleep is a deformed one. Adhering to the Ovidian text (*Metamorphoses* xi), Icelos takes on a snakelike neck with a goat's head on it, Morpheus appears as a satyr, and Sleep lodges a monstrous face on a gigantic nude lying down amid the symbols of dream. The artwork is a rather theatrical representation of the grotesque House of Sleep. Elsewhere, the *Mascherata* or *Trionfo dei sogni* for the wedding of Francesco de' Medici and Giovanna d'Austria (1566) centered on a *carro allegorico* drawn by *Quiete* and *Silenzio.* On it an elephant's head housed the realm of Sleep. Around it Morpheus wore the four faces of the ages of man, Icelos carried animal guises, and Phantaso spread out into a floral meadow with water, fire, and a little mountain. Surrounded as they were by grotesque decorations and a crowd of satyrs, they all agreed that desires are foolish and dreams are vain. As a lesson, people were to follow nature rather than art, which, however, could spell a powerful lure at night. Only at dawn would nature and the world of the spiritual sun reappear.

40. In Emma Spina Barelli's, *Teorici e scrittori d'arte tra Manierismo e Barocco* (Milan, 1966), 18; Baxter Hathaway, *The Age of Criticism: The Late Renaissance in Italy,* 375; Carlo Ossola, *L'Autunno del Rinascimento* (Florence, 1971), 207–13.

41. *The Social History of Art,* vol. 2 (New York, 1964), 103.

42. André Breton, in *Surrealists on Art,* 53.

43. In *Manifestoes of Surrealism,* (Ann Arbor, 1977), 302.

44. See Geoffrey Harpham, *On the Grotesque: Strategies of Contradictions in Art and Literature* (Princeton, 1962), xx–xxi; Peter Stallybrass and Allen White, *The Politics and Poetics of Transgression* (London, 1986).

Chapter 5

1. C. O. Brink, *Horace on Poetry,* vol. 2 (Cambridge, 1971), 81.

2. See E. H. Gombrich's references in *Norm and Form: Studies in the Art of The Renaissance* (London, 1971), 84–85, where he sets up the contrast between classical and nonclassical. Mikhail Bakhtin instead sets up the contrast between classical and grotesque, in *Rabelais and His World,* trans. Helen Iswolsky (Cambridge, Mass., 1968), 30.

3. See G. A. Gilio, *Trattati d'arte del Cinquecento* (Bari, 1962), 2:17–19; Cardinal Paleotti, in *Trattati,* 2:445. Also Michael Levey, *Early Renaissance* (Harmondsworth, Middlesex, 1967), 18; Nicole Dacos, *La découverte de la Domus Aurea et la formation des grotesques à la Renaissance* (London, 1969), 122–28; E. H. Gombrich, *The Heritage of Apelles* (Ithaca, N.Y., 1976), 57.

4. Geoffrey Harpham, *On the Grotesque: Strategies of Contradiction in Art and Literature* (Princeton, 1982), 27.

5. On Cellini, see G. C. Argan, *Storia dell'arte italiana,* vol. 3 (Florence, 1972), 139–40. On Pulci, see A. Bartlett Giamatti, *Exile and Change in Renaissance Literature* (New Haven, 1984), 44–48. For the dialectic of large forms coming out of small ones, see Jurgis Baltrusaitis, *Le moyen âge fantastique* (Paris, 1968), 57. Also Gaston Bachelard, *The Poetics of Space* (New York, 1964), 108–9.

6. *On Longing: Narratives of the Miniature, the Gigantic, the Souvenir, the Collection* (Baltimore, 1984), 66–69, 96.

7. *On the Grotesque: Strategies of Contradiction in Art and Literature,* 13–14.

8. See Edoardo Taddeo, "I grilli poetici di un pittore: le *Rime* di G.P. Lomazzo," in *Ideologia e scrittura nel Cinquecento* (Urbino, 1977), 147–48.

9. Ezio Raimondi's comment on Tasso, in *Poesia come retorica* (Florence, 1980), 61.

10. In this connection, Geoffrey Harpham notes that the grotesque "accommodates the things left over when the categories of language" have been exhausted, in *On the Grotesque: Strategies of Contradiction in Art and Literature,* 3. Also Renato Barilli, *Poetica e retorica* (Milan, 1969), 126–36; Giancarlo Mazzacurati, *Misure del classicismo rinascimentale* (Naples, 1967), 224.

11. *This Is Not a Pipe* (Berkeley, 1982), 54.

12. *The Monstrous Races in Medieval Art and Thought* (Cambridge, 1981), 35.

13. "Lectures on the Age of Elizabeth" (1820), in *Works,* vol. 6 (London, 1930), 192. Nietzsche, Section Four of his preface to *The Birth of Tragedy;* also Patricia Merivale, *Pan the Goat-God: His Myth in Modern Times* (Cambridge, Mass., 1969). In Venetian manuscript illuminations of the late fifteenth century, satyrs either played music or decorated initials and grotesque designs. See Lynn F. Kaufmann, *The Noble Savage: Satyrs and Satyr Families in Renaissance Art* (Ann Arbor, 1984), 45, 83–85.

14. In *The Earthly Republic: Italian Humanists on Government and Society,* ed. B. G. Kohl and R. G. Witt (Philadelphia, 1978), 246–47, 281. Also Paul Zumthor, *Langue, Texte, Enigme* (Paris, 1975), 54, 84, 38–41.

15. See François Rigolot, *Les langages de Rabelais* (Geneva, 1972), 34; Emile Pons, "Les 'Jargons' de Paniurge dans Rabelais," *Revue de littérature comparée* 2 (1931): 193–94. Jean Paris refers to "*mots-monstres,*" in *Rabelais au Futur* (Paris, 1970), 59–61.

16. *Allegory and the Migration of Symbols* (London, 1977), chaps. 3 and 4.

17. Mario Praz, *Il giardino dei sensi* (Vicenza, 1975), 25–32.

18. Proem to the second *Trattato,* in *Scritti scelti di Pietro Aretino e di Anton Francesco Doni,* ed. Giuseppe Guido Ferrero (Turin, 1962), 427. Translation mine. For a complete edition, see *La libraria,* ed. Gilito (Venice, 1550 and 1551). Also Amedeo Quondam and Giulio Ferroni, *La "locuzione artificiosa": Teoria ed esperienza della lirica a Napoli nell'età del manierismo* (Rome, 1973), 427–30. Also Amedeo Quondam, "La letteratura in tipografia," in *Letteratura italiana,* vol. 2, 630, refers to spaces of "artifice, paradox, and deceit"; Clayton Koelb, *The Incredulous Reader: Literature and the Function of Disbelief* (Ithaca, 1984), 55; François Rigolot, *Le Texte de la Renaissance: Des Rhétoriqueurs à Montaigne* (Droz, 1982), 54; Jean-Claude Margulin, "Mathias Ringmann's *Grammatica figurata,* or, Grammar as a Card Game," *Yale French Studies* 47 (1972): 33–46.

19. See Michel Leiris, *Mimologiques* (Paris, 1967), 90–91, 108–9; Praz, *Il giardino dei sensi,* 30; Robert Hardison, *Eccentric Spaces* (New York, 1977), 74–79; Mirelle Calle-Gruber, "Anamorphoses textuelles: Les écarts de la lettre dans le *Glossaire* de Michel Leiris," *Poétique* 42 (1980): 234–35; I. A. Richards, *How to Read a Page* (New York, 1942), 66.

20. *Watt* (New York, 1970), 165–68.

21. See Susan Stewart, *Nonsense: Aspects of Intertextuality in Folklore and Literature* (Baltimore, 1979), 62; Wendy Steiner's chapters "Nonsense and the Plain Style" and "The Nonsense Contradiction," in her *The Colors of Rhetoric* (Chicago, 1982); *Samuel Beckett: The Art of Rhetoric,* ed. E. Morot, H. Harper, and D. McMillan (Chapel Hill, 1976), 189–200; William J. Samarin, *Tongues of Men and Angels* (New York, 1972).

22. See Quondam and Ferroni, *La "locuzione artificiosa,"* 17.

23. Aldo Scaglione, "Cinquecento Mannerism and the Uses of Petrarch," *Medieval and Renaissance Studies* 5 (1969): 134.

24. Text and comments in Carlo Ossola's *L'Autunno del Rinascimento* (Florence, 1971), 200–203.

25. As an experimental stand against the expected, craftsmanship prevailed. In the arts, the styles of Michelangelo and Raphael inspired idealization. But there were parodies of the sculptural *David* perpetrated by Baccio Bandinelli (*Hercules*) and Ammannato Ammannati (*Neptune*). Verging on the preposterous, the artificiality of Buontalenti's *grotto* in the Boboli Gardens took on its own unnaturalness when Michelangelo's *Captives* were put there. While Leonardo's *facetie* (a genre that attracted scholars such as Bracciolini and Politian) mocked humanist seriousness, Titian "aped" the *Laocoön* in a woodcut, which also was meant to ape those who imitated his style. See Paul Barolsky, *Infinite Jest: Wit and Humor in Italian Renaissance Art* (Columbia, Mo., 1978), especially the chapter "Mannerist Bizzarrie," 101–38; Martin Kemp, *Leonardo da Vinci: The Marvellous World of Man and Nature* (Cambridge, Mass., 1981), 156.

26. See Claude-Gilbert Dubois, *Le Maniérisme* (Paris, 1979), 108. As to the irregularity of such linguistic creation, Gustav René Hocke draws a fundamental distinction between the seventeenth and twentieth centuries. In the earlier period, *licenza* still operated within an aesthetic system, which disintegrated into an absolute zero (*Nullpunkt*) with the Dadaists and their imitators, in *Manierismus in der Literatur* (Hamburg, 1959), 40.

27. *A Rhetoric of Motives* (New York, 1950), 45; *Permanence and Change* (Los Altos, Calif., 1964), 112–14.

28. Etienne Gilson writes that "le langage est en fait une tour de Babel, la confusion de la langue est la langue: et le travail du lexicographe est un effort pour sortir de cette confusion plutôt que pour l'accroître"; in *Linguistique et Philosophie* (Paris, 1969), 298–99.

29. See Paolo Santarcangeli, *Il libro dei labirinti* (Florence, 1967), 64.

30. J. Hillis Miller, "Ariadne's Thread: Repetition and the Narrative Line," *Critical Inquiry* 3/1 (1976): 70.

31. In the *précieux* language, the goddess would not comb her hair but would "*délabyrinthiser les cheveux*." The anatomical mosaic exudes fragrant breaths as lodestones (*aimant*) that attract words into a language at the edge of surrealist *champs magnétiques*. In the province of Mannerism instead, the grotesque magnet would attract the dismembered worlds of language and mimesis. See Claude-Gilbert Dubois, *Le Maniérisme* (Paris, 1979), 63; Gustav René Hocke, *Die Welt als Labyrinth* (Hamburg, 1957), 103; Praz, *Il giardino dei sensi*, 50. Jean Adhemar reaches the following conclusion with regard to Ronsard's poetry: "Les poésies de Ronsard sont pénétrées de l'esprit du Primatice. Pour lui les femmes ne sont pas des êtres vivants, des êtres de chair, mais des statues ou des peintures comme il en voit autour de lui"; in "Ronsard et l'Ecole de Fontainebleau," *Gazette des Beaux-Arts* 34 (1958): 23. Commenting on a similar poem by Guy de Tours, Gisele Mathieu-Castellani writes that, "comme chez Arcimboldo, où fleurs et fruits composent un visage 'naturalise,' l'objet est composé d'autres objets"; in "*D'un sein maniériste*," *Revue de littérature comparée* 56 (1982): 371–72. On Villa Demidoff as the mannerist *locus*, see Claudia Conforti, "Pratolino: Il giardino come mito della conoscenza e alfabeto figurato dell'immaginario," in *La città effimera e l'universo artificiale del giardino*, ed. Marcello Fagiolo (Rome, 1980), 183–92.

32. Umberto Eco, *Semiotics and the Philosophy of Language* (Bloomington, 1984), 88, 217.

33. See Samuel Kinser, *Rabelais's Carnival: Text, Context, Metatext* (Berkeley and Los Angeles, 1990), x.

Chapter 6

1. *The Gods Made Flesh: Metamorphosis and the Pursuit of Paganism* (New Haven, 1986), 73–75.

2. See Roberto Calasso, *Le nozze di Cadmo e Armonia* (Milan, 1988), 24–25.

3. In his preface to Françoise Frontisi-Ducroux's *Dédale: Mythologie de l'artisan en Grèce ancienne* (Paris, 1975), 10–11.

4. See Frontisi-Ducroux, *Dédale,* 89–90.

5. See illustration and comments in Leonard Cottrell, *The Bull of Minos* (New York, 1953), 132–33. Also R. F. Willetts, *The Civilization of Ancient Crete* (Berkeley, 1977), 106–7.

6. "Ariadne's Thread: Repetition and the Narrative Line," 62.

7. See Charles S. Baldwin, *Ancient Rhetoric and Poetic* (New York, 1924), 135.

8. *The Motives of Eloquence: Literary Rhetoric in the Renaissance* (New Haven, 1976), 2; Werner Jaeger, *Paideia: The Ideals of Greek Culture,* vol. 2 (Oxford, 1944), 144.

9. See Wilbur S. Howell, *Poetics, Rhetoric, and Logic: Studies in the Basic Disciplines of Criticism* (Ithaca, N.Y., 1975), especially 49–53.

10. *The Motives of Eloquence: Literary Rhetoric in the Renaissance,* 2–6.

Index